Dedication

To the entire McKeown and Kelly Families.
(My mother's and father's side of the family)

They have all stood there with me and I with them, as we seek the truth and continue our fight for our God-given freedoms.

The Electoral College 4 Dummmies?

Would it be better to simply count the popular vote?

In this book, you will learn about the purpose of the Electoral College and be able to come to your own conclusions about whether the Founders were all wet in the late 1700's and we now need to revert back to the popular vote. In 2016, Hillary Clinton won the Popular vote yet Donald Trump won the presidency. Therefore, many of the political left are crying foul. In 2000, when George Bush was elected president without winning the popular vote the same cry was heard.

Neither of these were as bad as in 1824, when John Quincy Adams was elected president despite not winning either the popular vote or the electoral vote. How could this be? Andrew Jackson was the clear winner in both categories. Jackson's popular vote total was 38,000 more than Adams. Moreover, Jackson beat Adams in the electoral vote 99 to 84. Despite being victorious, Jackson did no win the presidency. Why?

Andrew Jackson did not reach the majority 131 votes needed in the Electoral College to be declared president. Neither candidate did. So, what happened? The decision was made by the House of Representatives. It was the House—the People's Representatives, which voted Adams into the White House.

There were only two other stories like these. In 1876, Rutherford B. Hayes won the election by a margin of just one electoral vote; but he lost the popular vote by more than 250,000 ballots to Samuel J. Tilden. In 1888, Benjamin Harrison received 233 electoral votes to Grover Cleveland's 168, winning the presidency. Harrison lost the popular vote by more than 90,000 votes.

Why is this? When U.S. citizens go to the polls to "elect" a president, they are in fact voting for a particular slate of electors, though they vote for a properly named presidential candidate. In almost every state, the candidate who wins the most votes (that is, a plurality) in the state receives all the state's electoral votes. These are electoral votes based on the popular votes.

Why is this? You bought this book to find out. Is it a good or is it a bad idea? Is there any rhyme or reason to it? Were the Founders out on a bender the night before they made this decision or was the Electoral College a stroke of genius?

This is your best book to discover the answer and for understanding the current system and other possible systems to determine the presidency fairly.

Just because powerful people choose to ignore our rights and freedoms does not mean we must endure tyranny. The first step of course is to understand the most basic written precepts in the Constitution. Understanding the role of the Electoral College in our Constitution is of prime importance. Reading this book is a must.

BRIAN W. KELLY

Copyright © 2016 Brian W. Kelly .... Editor: Brian P. Kelly
The Electoral College 4 Dummmies Author Brian W. Kelly

Referenced Material : *Standard Disclaimer:* The information in this book has been obtained through personal and third Party observations, interviews, and copious research. Where unique information has been provided or extracted from other sources, those sources are acknowledged within the text of the book itself or at the end of the chapter in the Sources Section. Thus, there are no formal footnotes nor is there a bibliography section. Any picture that does not have a source was taken from various sites on the Internet with no credit attached. If resource owners would like credit in the next printing, please email publisher.

Published by:	LETS GO PUBLISH!
Editor	Brian P. Kelly ....
Email:	info@letsgopublish.com
Web site	www.letsgopublish.com

LETS GO PUBLISH!

Library of Congress Copyright Information Pending
Book Cover Design by Michele Thomas,

Acknowledgments are available for viewing at www.letsgopublish.com **at the bottom of the main menu..**

ISBN Information: The International Standard Book Number (ISBN) is a unique machine-readable identification number, which marks any book unmistakably. The ISBN is the clear standard in the book industry. 159 countries and territories are officially ISBN members. The Official ISBN for this book: **978-0-9982683-7-8**

The price for this work is:								**$12.99 USD**	
10	9	8	7	6	5	4	3	2	1

Release Date: December 2016

Acknowledgments

In every book that I write or edit, I publicly acknowledged all of the help that I have received from many sources. Some of these wonderful people are still on earth and others have made their way to heaven.

I would like to thank many people for helping me in this effort. I appreciate all the help that I received in putting this book together, along with the 66 other books from the past.

My printed acknowledgments were once so large that book readers needed to navigate too many pages to get to page one of the text. To permit me more flexibility, I put my acknowledgment list online at www.letsgopublish.com. The list of acknowledgments continues to grow. Believe it or not, it once cost about a dollar more to print so many pages in each book.

Thank you all on the big list in the sky and God bless you all for your help.

Please check out www.letsgopublish.com to read the latest version of my heartfelt acknowledgments updated for this book. Thank you all!

Special Acknowledgements to Benjamin Arthur Kelly, a fine young man, of canine descent, and an everyday participant in the book building process until he passed to the Lord a week ago. He never missed a day of work. Ben, I am sure would like to acknowledge his buddies Wylie Ky Eyelie, Angel Punkie Daniels, and Budmund (Buddy the Cat) Arthur Kelly. Some are dead and some are living but in my life, I've loved them all. They all deserve special tribute in the creation of this work.

.

Preface

We are citizens of a truly exceptional country. America is the exception to all rules for forming governments. Our country is founded on principles of liberty and freedom. It is the first government ever to elect officials who are subject to the people. The rule is of, by, and for the people, not of, by and for the government. All of the very powerful officials in all forms of governments—local, state, and national—work for the people.

The Founders knew that even the great Constitution they wrote might not be enough to keep knaves and scoundrels from subverting their work.

And so, today, over 225 + years after the Constitution, all is not perfect in America, but the principles of the Constitution are so sound and so powerful that even a knave politician cannot bring us under. The big concern of course is that if we don't smarten up, things can and will get a lot worse. I suspect that is why you are reading this book.

How could such wise men have created a system in a representative Republic in which the popular vote does not determine the president? There are lots of reasons but suppose Pennsylvania was so prosperous it had 51% of the voters. What would happen if year-in and year-out, all 100% of the PA citizens-- 51 % (majority)—each and every one voted in the general election for their favorite candidate? Would it matter what California or New York wanted? No, it would not.

Our country's ailments are large and growing. Taxes are too high; elected officials are out of touch; government is too big, spending is out of control; the new healthcare program is a train wreck, the federal government is incompetent; the people seem to have no voice in government; too many people are too lazy to hold government accountable, too many are on the take, and worse than that, the list of ailments is growing, not shortening. The losers in every election cry foul when the Constitution is followed. Some are willing to cast the Constitution, our guarantee from tyranny, aside so that their guy can win an election. Then what?

Your intention no doubt in learning about the structure of America and its most fundamental laws is to figure out how a mechanism such as an Electoral College, can determine a presidency. Yet, most do not complain that the number of representatives in the House of representatives is not equal and in fact favors the states with higher populations.

By choosing to read this book, you have decided that you want to understand why what is happening regarding elections is happening. Thank you. That is why Brian wrote the book.

Sooner or later, you will better understand our great country and our great form of government—at least before the bad guys take it away.

If you have been paying attention to what is going on in America today, you know we are in trouble. We have a busted economy, high unemployment, no jobs, and our basic rights to freedoms such as speech, religion, the press, and our right-to-bear-arms are being impinged upon.

The Founders saw it as a civic duty for Americans to pay attention to our government so that we can avoid being chumps and being snookered by crooked politicians. That is why you are reading this book.

There are more issues than just those noted above, and we better fix them quickly while we still have a Constitution upon which to lean.

We are on the same side in this battle for the Constitution and for the survival of America. Together we can all help. We first must understand what is going on and we then must understand our rights as delivered in the Declaration of Independence, The Constitution, and the Bill of Rights.

Nobody suggests that we simply take it on the chin and forget that we may be harmed by government policies even if they are constitutional. Though not a living document, the Constitution can be amended when it is proven wrong. The people again get to decide by voting whether to change the Constitution. That is the beauty of our government. Our Constitution, by the way, has been changed (amended) twenty-seven times.

Among other things, this book will help you understand why the Founders chose to have an Electoral College and put you in a position to understand whether that is best for all of America or not. If not, of course, then your duty would be to work to have a Constitutional Amendment brought forth to the people for approval.

Your author continually monitors what is happening to our government and he has written extensively on the major problems our country faces. Brian Kelly is one of America's most outspoken and eloquent nationalist spokesmen.

He is the author of America 4 Dummmies, The Bill of Rights 4 Dummmies, The Annual Guest Plan, Saving America, Taxation Without Representation, Kill the EPA!, Jobs! Jobs! Jobs! The Federalist Papers by the Framers, and many other patriotic books. All books are available at www.amazon.com/author/brianwkelly.

Brian W. Kelly has read the founding documents, the underlying intelligence reports, and he has researched and written about such topics for years. Brian has written ninety-five books and hundreds of patriotic articles.

He is deeply concerned about how intolerable the results of poor government policy can be within our neighborhoods and our lives. His comprehensible and sane recommendations in this book are explained in detail within the covers of this soon-to-be classic edition.

You are going to love this book since it is designed by an American for Americans. Few books are a must-read but The Electoral College 4 Dummmies is destined to quickly appear at the top of America's most read list.

Sincerely,

Brian P. Kelly, Editor

Table of Contents

About the Author

Brian W. Kelly retired as an Assistant Professor in the Business Information Technology (BIT) program at Marywood University, where he also served as the IBM i and midrange systems technical advisor to the IT faculty. Kelly designed, developed, and taught many college and professional courses. He is a contributing technical editor to a number of IT industry magazines. On the Patriotic side, you can find many of Kelly's article on www.brianwkelly.com.

Kelly is a former IBM Senior Systems Engineer and he has been a candidate for US Congress and the US Senate from Pennsylvania. He has an active information technology consultancy. He is the author of 95 books and numerous articles. Ask Brian to speak at your next rally! You would enjoy his frank perspectives!

Over the past twenty years, Brian Kelly has become one of America's most outspoken and eloquent conservative / nationalist protagonists. Brian loves America. Besides The Electoral College 4 Dummmies, Kelly is also the author of many other patriotic books. Check them out at www.Amazon.com/author/brianwkelly, bookhawkers.com, Kindle, and other fine booksellers.

Chapter 1 The Electoral College is Under Attack—Good or Bad?

Did the Founders make a mistake?

In November 2016, the many fine supporters of Hillary Clinton for President were very upset that she was not the President-elect. Many on the right were similarly upset similarly four years prior in November 2012. Despite their being some people in the dumps about Hillary, there was another substantial group that were very pleased that Donald Trump was going to be inaugurated as the 45th President. Not all people are feeling good but then again, they never are.

The Electoral College is one of the attack points for Democrats today. Those who love Hillary Clinton want the notion thrown out as the proper way to determine the election of a president. Whether the Electoral College is a good method or not, it was the agreed upon procedure in which both candidates agreed to participate in the—shall we say—presidential election games.

Scholars on both sides of the political spectrum for months were busy checking everything out to assure posterity and today's good Americans, that this was probably a simple Founders' afterthought or perhaps some heavy eighteenth century thinking had gone astray. They stumble, however, when they find that the foundation of the Electoral College, in fact, is embodied, part and parcel within the US Constitution.

For the inquisitive mind, one must look into Article 2, Section 1 for the original writing. Then, to get it right for today, one must check out the 12th Amendment to the Constitution as well as the 20th Amendment. We will do this in this book.

For now, Never Trumpers and Hillary Supporters, are both whining that the selection method is unfair. They wonder "Why did the Founders do this to us?"

Well, Democrats are very concerned about the founding because to them the Founders conspired 225 years ahead of time to eliminate Hillary Clinton from taking office on January 20, 2017. Now, Don't you think that is such a dirty trick that only a god could have pulled it off?

History suggests that the Founders' intention in assuring that a great president would be elected every four years, was also to inhibit the possibility that n'ere do wells or insurgents or leaders of other countries could become the US President by a fluke or a national miscount.

In 2016, why is the Electoral College a question?

The rumor mill produces some great rumors. Many rumors are the truth packaged as a rumor. Few people seem willing to take credit for starting most rumors. As the days and weeks went by from the election on, Americans got more and more fed up with an election that is supposed to be over according to the rules. What rules you may ask? The rules that both candidates agreed to use to determine the winner. Nonetheless, the disputes persist but the Constitution insists: "Ignore them."

One of the rumors du jour is that Hillary Clinton did not plan to concede but was convinced to do so by then President Barack Hussein Obama. Perhaps he knew it would be futile or perhaps he did not want anything to mess up a clean transition for legacy purposes. Your call on that folks.

Nonetheless for the first two weeks after the election, the liberal media complained incessantly that former Secretary of State Hillary Clinton had won the popular vote, which ignores the existence of state populations and state governments, and states as sovereign entities.

They also complained that Donald Trump, the winner under the rules of engagement, and today's President-elect according to the universe of Democratic Leadership, should concede to Hillary Clinton over the popular vote.

As recently as two weeks after the election the mainline pundits, especially Politico, ran stories that Clinton's lead in the popular vote had surpassed 2 million votes — but Trump still held the advantage in the Electoral College. Dah! The rules that Hillary Clinton agreed to said that only the Electoral College matters.

The typical liberal response to disturbing news that may hurt them in any way—even if they deserve to be hurt in a particular scenario—is to create a national problem and try to hurt somebody else. They are doing that as I am writing this analysis of the Electoral College as the proper means to select our presidential candidates. Hey, our intellectual Founders worked it out 225 years ago! Why not a peep til now?

The liberal progressive nay-sayers on the election "think" this election is invalid simply because Hillary Clinton was not elected president. The next step for loyal liberal progressive socialists was that they had to find some reason why the election was invalid—even if there were no real reason.

Since they could not say the results were "trumped up" as this idea might favor their opponent, they had to pick on the lowly Electoral College, a notion the Founders spent much time deciding was best for America and Americans.

The Founders were so impressed with the notion that after considering many other fair ideas, they settled on the Electoral College. Hillary supporters would be happy to eliminate the whole Constitution to have the Electoral College notion changed to the popular vote. But, thankfully, that is not going to

4 The Constitution 4 Dummmies!

happen. Some scholars suggest that even if it were changed, the elimination of the millions of illegal votes from Moonbeam Brown's Calfornia would bring the results back to where they are at this time.

By now, enough time has passed as you are reading this book, this year's elections are history. Nonetheless, this book takes you through the rationale for both Hillary R. Clinton and Donald J Trump to have originally agreed to play by the same rules. Were they kidding with each other? Or just as Mitt Romney and other RINOS, was it just Hillary who was kidding when she shook hands and agreed to come out fighting?

My favorite talk radio host of all time is Rush Limbaugh. He is as good as he says he is. He gets it right 99.97% of the time so I do always seek his position on major issues. He does see a situation in which duly announced President-elect Donald Trump might not have won the popular vote. However, Limbaugh adds "but he would have won it if he had needed to win' Amen to that notion! In other words, if Trump had agreed to a different set of rules, he would have won under those rules.

Supporters of Democrat Hillary Clinton have been claiming that she has won the popular vote from the day Hillary stopped lamenting her loss and finally assumed her natural disposition – anger.

The Hillarian supporters now suggest that Trump does not have a full mandate to pursue his agenda. But what Limbaugh said on his show demonstrated that Donald Trump had not focused on winning the popular vote. He focused on the rules of engagement agreed to by his opponent.

Since the Hillary-preferred, post-facto change is not how the race was permitted to be decided, one can wonder would her non-agreement to the original terms have made a difference? But, she agreed!

First of all, the Constitution would not have permitted it. The other major fact is that Hillary Rodham Clinton agreed to abide by terms laid out by the Constitution of the United States of America. She made a big fuss in the final debate about how she would follow the letter of the law and not contest it. Yet, here she is caught in another lie.

What did the handshake between the candidates mean?

Trump decided to attempt to win the presidency under the terms of his handshake with Hillary Clinton. Even in a prize fight, the boxers agree that the decisions of the referees and the judges are binding.

Limbaugh and many others speculate that if the Electoral College did not exist, "It would have made states like New York and California automatically in play," Everybody checking out the news knew that both California and New York, with massive electoral votes were all going to Hillary using the Electoral College System. Hillary did not complain about getting all these electoral votes once. This was a big deficit from which the Trump folks began their campaign vote count.

Regarding whether California and New York were in play that Trump should attempt to sway their thinking, reality suggests that they were so far into Hillary's camp nobody in his or her right mind would find them changing to Trump under the Electoral System. So, this helped Hillary Clinton. It kept Donald Trump from being active in "her" states.

Mr. Trump therefore did not spend any time in California, and he spent very little time in New York because there was no point. He had no chance to win these states under Electoral College rules but he could have gotten a lot more votes if he landed the Trump Plane in a few Golden State cities and had a few major rallies in the state.

If he were trying to collect individual voters (popular vote strategy) instead of being forced to win the state (Electoral College strategy), the plan would have been much different and the vote count would have been much different. Rules matter, especially those in which both Parties agree before the count.

Trump lovers in California and New York may have been upset at Trump's lack of attention to their state and they may have gone for Hillary just for being ignored. So, logic dictates that if Trump had campaigned in these states, the popular vote would have been substantially less in favor of his opponent. It stands the true test of logical reasoning.

Even if every Republican in both states voted for the GOP nominee, there still would be no chance of it going red, Limbaugh said. But, there were lots of Democrats across the USA who had had enough of big government and so in frustration, they voted for Trump.

Can we not speculate that if the handshake battle were fought with different rules, the different rules may have produced different outcomes. Why is it a bad thing that the agreed upon rules prevailed and the legitimate winner under the agreed upon rules is now the declared winner. We know him as President Elect Donald J. Trump? I could not be more pleased.

How much whining by the kid who always took his ball home, when he did not get his way, is the American public going to withstand as a nation? It is time for Democrats to take the medicine they so enjoy dishing out.

My neighbors, a mix of both D & R are sick of the whining! Real Americans are tough competitors. When we lose, we dust off our sandals and go at it again. We don't cry!

A friendly neighborhood Democrat showed me his new perception of his Party—the picture above. Is this not the proper reflection of a Party that would rather whine than play by the rules. There has been little truth in the Democratic Party for many years. As a Democrat, I know many in my Party cannot even count. So, why recount?

The big deal is that when the Democrats were trying to slam the Republicans for being liars (Think about how absurd that is), they came up with the best Republican word takedown ever. They said that Republicans cannot recognize the TRUTH. They then added that Republicans think that TRUTH is just another of the four-letter words they hate.

The COUNT from Sesame Street needed to be called by the Hillary Campaign in to settle this small dispute. He took over th conversation. He said: I am the COUNT. I Love to Count. One makes me happy... Two makes me better... by the time he reached five on the word truth in the four-letter word quiz, The COUNT was done. Hey Democrats, forget about bringing in big personalities to verify your falsehoods. Why not stick to the truth? Then even the COUNT will be happy with the count.

Nobody likes being depicted as the whiner on the prior page. How about just telling the truth.

As a former Democrat lover who today is just a registered Democrat, I say the Party has become the Party of cry-babies and nothing matters unless D's win. As a white guy, I wonder why do Democratic leaders hate whites so much? Who's ever asked that question before? If I am white and I figure Democrats hate me, what is my natural response in the voting booth?

Whatever happened to the notion of doing things for the good of the country? What happened to that idea being the overriding credo? I ran for office formally twice and informally once. I lost every time I ran as a Democrat because I am not a suck-up to the Democratic Party.

I loved calling myself a JFK Democrat, which I am. "Ask not what your country can do for you but ask rather what you can do for your country?"

That was the JFK way. Today's Democrats would put JFK and his thoughts about America out onto the trash heap of history. Not me!

This is despite JFK being one of the finest of Americans.

The big question for the Democrats today is that if Trump had won the popular vote by the exact number claimed by the Democrats, and he had lost the presidency via the agreed upon method, would all Democrats be rioting because Trump had been denied the presidency?

Or is it possible that this is all politics, and the dirtiest politics of all—politics that undermine the fundamental goodness of the United States of America.

Should we ask where the funding for the dissent from the Constitution and the decrees of the Founders comes from? Who is funding the pro-Hillary rallies / riots? Is the money coming from a John F Kennedy fund or from his now liberal, socialist, progressive family?

Or is it possibly from a non-American who hates America. Can the support for un-American activities come directly from George Soros, a man who has love of money and lots of money but who has no love for any of the countries of the world, especially the U. S. of A. Can this be? Would Jill Stein still have money left it were not for Uncle George?

Either way, the Democratic Party as run by the alt-left in this country, or the plain-left (AKA the Democratic Party) will not decide overnight to behave as patriotic Americans.

The people need to take over their media or their asininity will infect the minds of the mush brained millennials who 100% buy into their stinky spew.

Chapter 2 The Electoral College; the Popular Vote, and Fairness

Is the Electoral College fair to Americans?

Rush Limbaugh has really taken on the notion of the Electoral College. Much of the thought part seems to be coming from universities funded by the rest of us. Rush wonders how the attacks can be deemed fair? His opinion more than likely mirrors my own: "Why would we think America's best intellectuals have brains when all they put out is poison?" These communist coffee breath professors spew their crap in the classroom and then brag about their drivel and the effects on our children in the faculty lounges.

"What if there were no Electoral College?" Rush said. "[In the 2016 general election] You wouldn't have had nearly as much time spent in North Carolina. You wouldn't have had nearly as much time spent in Wisconsin by Trump or Michigan or Ohio or some of these Rust Belt states."

"You would have Trump going where the people were. He would have gone to New York. He would have gone to California. He may not have needed to win the state, but if the popular vote were all that counted, he could have easily won this election by simply changing focus."

That said, Limbaugh said he expects Trump will end up winning this year's popular vote anyway once all votes are finally counted.

He said he believes a "significant number" of illegal immigrants voted.

"I wouldn't be surprised if the number is as high as two million illegal immigrants."

Rush Limbaugh is not the only concerned American about whether illegal foreign nationals have usurped the American citizen-only right of voting.

Months before the election, Barack Hussein Obama openly counseled illegal foreign nationals that they could and should vote with impunity in the election. Jerry Brown of California legalized the illegal vote. Many are wondering how many illegal foreign nationals actually took heed of American and State leaders to cast their vote against the wall?

The number could be as high as 3 million. When I first wrote this chapter, over 3.5 million had yet to vote in California. Where are the busses to the polls coming from? Guadalajara?

Now, when they do the recounts in some states where Jill Stein suggests are fraudulent, why not include all states? Why not challenge all of Hillary's narrow victories? Why? Because the whole thing is claptrap Democratic Politics, hoping Uncle Ben, the only guy in the family for Hillary can claim a victory soon.

Why not contest California and if the count is not done in time, the Golden State's 55 votes would be O-U-T and it would even out the fraud in MI, WI, and PA so Trump would be the elector victor. Why do we permit scoundrels to drive us to the brink?

Gregg Phillips is a founder of VoteStand (an APP for finding and reporting voter fraud), His Twitter profile notes that The Cause, Time for a Hero, Voters Trust & Winning Our Future PAC are big items as they should be. He tweeted some interesting observations and analyses:

"We have verified more than three million votes cast by non-citizens."

"We are joining .@TrueTheVote to initiate legal action."

Here is another tweet from Phillips:

"Completed analysis of database of 180 million voter registrations.

"Number of non-citizen votes exceeds 3 million.

"Consulting legal team."

Here is one more:

"We will expose all of our data to the public in order to show America the left's seedy underbelly. #unrigged"

Let's see what happens.

If Hillary had disavowed the illegitimate Jill Stein recount effort, this would be over now but Hillary wants to be President more than she wants to serve the interests of Americana.

Too bad!

Phillips has a few more observations:

"The problem is that at least 3 million illegals may have voted, and likely for Hillary. If they did, and the 3 million number is removed from the popular vote count, it would mean that Trump won the popular vote as well. Clinton was only ahead by 630,877 votes when this was written."

Is there a historical solution?

Unlike Burr and Hamilton, Hillary and Donald Trump chose not to choose their method of final resolution to a dispute. Hillary conceded and that was a gentleman's way to end a dispute. But, now she is back at it again like there was no concession! Maybe the Pardon ought to be off the table also.

Maybe the Hill-Trump dispute cannot be resolved peaceably. At least not yet. Politico is so interested in blood, I am awaiting their call for both candidates to agree to use American-made Smith & Wesson units to settle the dispute. Both ideas are absurd.

The biased, corrupt media chooses not to mention that the general election, by a prescription in the Constitution that has many great points, does not use the popular vote to determine the winner of the presidency.

They fail to mention that just like when the boxers touch gloves in a match, both Hillary Clinton and Donald Trump agreed to the terms of their match. Each of the two-general election presidential candidates (as if they were boxers duking it out) were well aware that they needed to get to 270 electoral votes to win. There was no secret plan. Loser buys!

On November 8, when Hillary Clinton was convinced that she had lost both the popular vote and the electoral vote, she went to bed and left her campaign manager, John Podesta, to clean up and tell the throngs waiting for her acceptance speech, who just wanted to see this historical lady, that she would not be showing up to say hello or anything else. I still do not have a respectable excuse for her dissing her own.

When Hillary knew she was doomed, there was no glad handing and hugging of staff or fans. I suspect that made a few Democrats very disappointed—perhaps as much as the loss. They had worked their way into the Party and the guest of honor was a no-show! No pics; No selfies!

Podesta sent them all home with unrequited love. Mrs. Clinton did not concede at this point. Rumor has it Barbara Streisand, on her way to Canada, popped in and when she saw nothing Clinton-positive, she popped right back out hoping to be unnoticed. But, Babs, a fine American (cough!) was spotted! Maybe she had a few consolation Manhattans with Hillary? Nobody knows! Maybe Hillary sang "Memories" for Babs!

There was also a reported Obama pep-talk for her to concede quickly. He and the world knew she had lost. The President wanted a peaceful, conciliatory transition of power so his future books would sell at a higher price and in larger numbers than in a nasty transition.

Was overnight Hillary all-alone?

When Hillary woke up realizing she was not the President-elect, I suspect that she was all-alone. Nobody wanted to be close-by—in harm's way. Getting whacked with a cup, a saucer, or a plate could ruin one's countenance. Nobody wanted to get whacked by a flying dish or an errant overcooked breakfast danish.

There was not enough spare football equipment available for all the staff to be fully protected. That did change things, however for Mrs. Clinton. It was a stark realization. It was over. She had lost. She had stiffed her fan base the night before and had mumbled a concession to Trump in the middle of her sleep.

When the wonderment of Manhattan Majestics wore off long after the fireworks were not set off, and the crushing realization headache started full bore, a few Advil may have helped. Being a smart lady, Mrs Clinton was convinced she had to do some things to avoid the stigma of appearing as sore loser forever. She had to be gracious. This night of sleep and a sleepy concession had changed things big-time.

She was reassured there was no reason to be concerned about being or not being pardoned or not being prosecuted in the Trump administration. She gave a great speech that everybody but I would have believed if I did not know her from her past. Yet, I admit it was well written and well-delivered. It would have been perfect if she left it there and did not pick up the torch again on the recounts and the popular vote total.

Now, in th emost recent days of this book coming to a close, with Jill Stein showing Mrs. Clinton the new light—the recount light to the presidency—Mrs. Clinton has again joined the foray, hoping God was not looking when she did the bad things.

She is ready again to be anointed to the presidency. She has decided to more or less take back her concession and piggyback on the Jill Stein recount.

To do this she must enlist a team of probable Soros-paid-intimidators to harass and threaten the regular Joes serving as electors, and to pay off the vote counters in the states that agree to let the Hillary programed vote re-counting machine in to determine the real winner. Who knows? Chicanery is a Clinton political art.

After the November 8 election, on Wednesday morning, early, Mrs. Clinton finally noticed that she had squeaked past Donald Trump in the national popular vote. Since then her lead appears to be increasing. It stood to reason her lead could actually grow as more popular vote results were reported, especially on the West Coast in places like California, where Republicans, they say, need to get a special permit just to walk the streets.

The hard facts had already determined that she had lost the election based on the agreed upon terms. But, she saw the light of day and another shot at winning the covered prize of her life – the presidency.

Rush Limbaugh has noted that we may find upon further investigation that the surplus of voters for Hillary may be of the illegal foreign national variety, but nobody is investigating that possibility as of yet. Jill Stein has piqued Hillary's Penchant for the dramatic.

What is for sure is that Jill Stein, a Green Party Candidate who has a right to a recount and who put the $3.5 million money up in Wisconsin to pay for it. Well, sort-of. She had fundraisers.

When Ms. Stein brought up the idea of a vote recount. The Hillary team jumped on it. So, Stein is paying for her own vote recount. Stein may even make a few million on the recount if it costs less than her estimates and the donors are kind.

Does anybody really think that it was a good acting job for the Clintonistas to show that it was only after extreme pressure that Mrs. Clinton agreed to support Stein's efforts in Michigan, Wisconsin, and Pennsylvania—three key states that Donald Trump narrowly won in the recent presidential election. I must admit that when Jill Stein initiated the recount. I felt that Clinton or Soros money or both was behind it. But, I have no facts.

I had a hard time believing that Mrs. Clinton, after her unity speech, conceding that America had done its best and had voted Donald Trump as president-elect, would try again to steal the election. She must have forgotten these lines from her speech of November 9, 2016:

"Donald Trump is going to be our president. We owe him an open mind and the chance to lead. Our constitutional democracy enshrines the peaceful transfer of power."

After such a splendid heartfelt unity speech, it did not seem like Mrs. Clinton would take back this great speech and join with a rogue third Party candidate to discredit the true and honest President-elect. But, she did, nonetheless.

Jill Stein, who ran for the presidency on the Green Party's ticket, when I wrote this paragraph had already raised close over $6 million in a crowdfunding campaign to initiate recounts in the three states. And, on Friday, weeks after the election, filed for one in Wisconsin. She paid $3.5 million for the Wisconsin recount. Pennsylvania is supposedly underway as is Michigan. We'll see. On December 1, 2016, she requested a recount in Michigan.

Donald Trump is undaunted. He fired off this tweet on November 27. "In addition to winning the Electoral College in a landslide, I won the popular vote if you deduct the millions of people who voted illegally."

On Saturday, November 26, less than three weeks after Hillary Clinton conceded, her campaign counsel, Mark Erik Elias said that Clinton would join the effort, though he noted that their own investigation had not turned up any evidence of tampering. A reversal of the results in those states could, in theory, tip the election to Hillary Clinton.

Does an apparently sincere concession with an apparently sincere wish for the future for President-elect Trump mean anything?

Does the official Constitutional final vote count matter?

Although the election was held way back on November 8, and the electors had been scheduled to vote for Trump on December 19, there were still states counting votes.

Many votes are of the absentee and provisional variety while some other states have yet to declare their tallies certified and official. As of Saturday (Nov. 25), Clinton was leading in the popular vote, 64.6 million to Trump's 62.4 million. Trump overwhelmingly won the Electoral College and is for all intents and purposes, the President-elect. It's not going to change.

I believe sincerely that if we asked all the people in the flyover states whether they would prefer to sit home on election day and let the general election tabulators count just California and New York, they would tell you where to go and quickly. BTW, I am pleased that PA is now a "flyover state."

Would the flyover 48 feel that democracy was served if only California and NY got to vote? Would that idea serve our nation well?

I would suggest that the other 48 states would by majority decide that the two most populous states with the most electoral votes could go to where the temperature is out of this world.

I think it is fair to say that if they could not win officially with such a commanding immediate majority of electors—New York's 29 votes, and California's 55, then the Democrats with such a head start do not deserve to win any election. Why can't the Democratic Party convince anybody else to vote Democrat? Why blame Hillary's loss on a few great patriots from the eighteenth century.

Email Wisdom

The Founders really did know what they were doing. Just a few days after I had finished my first draft of this book, I received this email from a friend. I have stripped off all the headers:

"Some of you already know this – some don't. Whether Democrat, Republican or Independent, here's something to think about:

We hear a cacophony of blaring and bleating from the media and the Hillary supporters that she won the popular vote and therefore she should be president, 60,839,497 to 60,265,847. 47.8% to 47,3% with the remaining 4.9% going to the other candidates. But here is a more in-depth analysis:

Trump won the popular vote in 31 states to her 19 and DC... 62% Trump to her 19%. Trump led in the total popular vote for all states except California. She won California 5,860,714 to his 3,151,821. 61.6% to 33.1% exclusive of the other candidates. Thus California gave Hillary the popular vote for all states as claimed by the Democrats and their media supporters.

But deduct her California vote from her national vote, it leaves her with 54,978,783, and deduct Trumps California vote from his national total, it leaves him with 57,113,976, he wins in a landslide in the total for the other 49 states, 51.3% to her 48.7%.

So, in effect, Hillary was elected president of California and Trump was elected president of the rest of the country by a substantial margin.

This exemplifies the wisdom of the Electoral College, to prevent the vote of any one populace state from overriding the vote of the others.

With our voter registration available when getting a driver's license combined with undocumented immigrants allowed driver's licenses we have no controls in place to keep non-citizens from voting.

So I ask you, frankly, do you REALLY want California voters to elect your presidents for you? Or any other heavily populated state? It would be like the tail wagging the dog. The average state has 8.7 members in the US House of Reps. If states weren't restricted to two senators each, CA would have 12.

If no Electoral College, candidates would only campaign probably only in CA and NY....all they'd need to win.

The founding fathers never cease to amaze me with their foresight and wisdom.
â€‹
They truly were extremely thoughtful and smart.

I agree.

Chapter 3 Americans Are Mad as Hell About An Elite Establishment.

Both Democrats & Republicans are upset

These are strange times indeed as a non-establishment, non-elitist candidate has emerged victorious and is now the President-elect.

Democrats are mad as hell that their candidate, Hillary Clinton supported by establishment elite Democrats, not including many white middle class voters, once the stronghold of Democrat politics, did not win according to plan. Democrats are beginning to notice a smugness in their Party starting with Bernie Sanders having been thrown under the bus in a purely corrupt move by the big-shots at the DNC. Regular Democrats such as I feel betrayed by our Party.

Republican regular guys, who are against the elite establishment in both Parties are very pleased with the election results. However, few are pleased with the establishment elites in the Republican Party trying to undermine their candidate.

Nationalists and populists and conservatives in both Parties brought forth Donald Trump. It is not a matter of Party. It is a matter of the people having gotten fed up with the status quo and the stench of corruption. Trump got a substantial portion of the Democratic ballots or he never could have won the electoral vote.

By the way, regarding the electoral vote, suddenly Jill Stein decided to create some hay by demanding a recount in three states—Michigan, Pennsylvania, and Wisconsin. Ironically, Stein originally thought she needed $1.5 million to get the recounts done. Yet, each time she reached the new higher reset goal, she always needed more. Donald Trump calls it a Green Party fundraiser. She received well over $6.7 million in donations.

Latest numbers have Ms. Stein now asking for about $9.5 million. Skeptical Trump supporters see this as another way to scam wounded and upset Democrats and the few Greens out there out of more money. It is another Democratic Fundraiser in cooperation with the Green Party. Despite the low probability of success, glum and moping Democratic elites, who have yet to resume normal lives after November 8, are writing checks in record numbers.

Nobody's word seems to mean anything anymore so why should Hillary Clinton's concession. Romney promised to support Trump, then damned Trump during the campaign, and now he is ready to support him again in exchange for a Cabinet Position. The Hillary team that graciously conceded on November 9 are now behaving as if on that day they were only kidding.

Donald Trump tweets it this way:

"Hillary Clinton conceded the election when she called me just prior to the victory speech and after the results were in. Nothing will change."

Why should it change? When it is over; it is over!

"The Democrats, when they incorrectly thought they were going to win, asked that the election night tabulation be accepted. Not so anymore!"

I agree. Do Democratic leaders think that we Democrats are stupid?

Apparently, in their minds Hillary Clinton, who already conceded, should be given another chance to steal a win. Therefore, all the grace of Mrs. Clinton's "Lets' unite behind Trump" concession speech has been spent. The grace is gone. Mrs. Clinton will have to go to Confession if the place doesn't melt on her arrival, in order to get some self-earned grace. But how much?

Elite Democrats who have been sulking since November 8, are now getting ready to resume their routine of lying and cheating and stealing regularly to help Hillary win the Michigan, Pennsylvania, and Pennsylvania recounts if they happen as Hill and Jill plan. Of course, they don't acknowledge their December 5, 2016 setback when Philadelphia's sample of 75 precincts brought Hillary just five new votes. The tweeters loved talking about the price per vote at $200,000.

The chance of overturning the result of the election is considered very slim, even if all three states go along with the recount. However, Mrs Clinton's lawyers could not resist the opportunity, especially with all the money being spent. So, concession smession—they have joined Ms. Stein's efforts.

Skeptics talk about all the ways that Hillary can steal the election and they all begin with her conceding the election. But they caution that the concession is just to catch the winning opponent off guard so that he and his millions of supporters think that it's in the bag, and so they don't prepare for recounts, lawsuits, or ballot challenges. This does seem to be happening.

They also suggest that Hillary might sit"innocently" by while her supporters publish the names and contact information for all electors and they begin a campaign to "persuade" them to not vote as they're ethically and morally supposed to vote. They suggest that it is very important to make them "faithless electors" by suggesting they can vote for someone else–anyone else as long as the electoral winner gets no electoral votes when they are cast. In this way, perhaps it would be Hillary, and not Donald who ends up with the majority of electoral votes actually cast.

Of course, to help in this effort, it would be great t have pals in the media willing to lie—these would be trusty friends, not from Fox News with whom Hillary may have colluded successfully in the past. Perhaps a few suggestions to the media to pen some nice juicy stories about Russians hacking the electronic machines and about the winning opponent being a white supremacist. All of this can establish an atmosphere in which the loser who chose not to address even her loyal supporters on election night might be able to steal the election from some babes in the woods who do not understand the politics of death.

Who knows what will happen? I do! Nothing! A deal is a deal! But, we all need to pay attention. If Donald Trump did not coin that phrase "A deal is a deal!" then Brian W. Kelly, noted author of 96 books, is ready to claim it as his own. I know the guy. Don't worry. He's OK!

Isn't it something that the Hillary Campi is again behaving in a fashion that turned off millions of Americans this year. Let me further tap into those feelings that have all ordinary Americans sick and tired of Washington Shenanigans and corruption.

Besides the cry that the vote is incorrect because of the Russians, the losers are also attacking the Electoral College as specified in the US Constitution. The Constitution of course is the most wonderful document in the world other than the Bible itself.

The Bible as we know was written by the hand of God, whereas the Constitution was written by the Founders of America, a group of men whose members would cry, "Give me Liberty or Give Me Death."

While many patriots died giving the US its birth and its freedom from tyrannical British rule, Democrats and the Green Party are now pushing that perhaps there is no validity to the Constitution. Before Donald Trump tweets on that one, let me say: "Perhaps there is no validity to the Democratic Party or the Green Party."

The Electoral College as specified in the Constitution, the Amendments, and the Federalist Papers have shown that in a presidential election, the people in the states determine elections rather than having them decided at an unaccountable national level.

Which among you wants Barack Obama counting all of this years' popular votes? Which among you wants Donald Trump counting the next election's ballots? Don't you want a system that prevents Barack when the Democrats run everything or Donald, when the Republicans run everything from determining who his successor is to be, without concern for the people?

Yes, all citizens of America are citizens of the US of A. But, before that they were born in Townships, Cities, Counties, States, and together as part of great United States of America, their Constitution speaks for them in an America designed for Americans.

Meanwhile Americans have been upset for most of the Obama years because from the outset, he and the Democrats have attacked our Constitution. Today's attack on the Electoral College, which we evaluate in this book, is part of many attacks. The Democratic Party is on record wanting government and not the people in America to hold the power cards. Fighting the notion of an Electoral College is just one of their many war tactics.

The Constitution, the law of the land which we explore in depth in this book regarding the Electoral College and its value, has been usurped by President Obama and the Democrats, especially in the immigration area. It has unlawfully been bypassed by opportunists in government during the Obama years. Democrats would be able to dupe the people far easier if there were no Constitution. No Constitution therefore is their goal.

That makes a lot of US "Mad as Hell!" I am mad as hell and many voters were mad as hell and that is why so many came out to vote for Donald Trump. Why would anybody of a conservative, nationalist, or populist ilk who loves America not be outraged.

Even as a Democrat, I feel the conservative Republican pain as I was supportive of less than 1 % of the Obama agenda. Yet, we nationalist populists were pushed around by Mitch McConnell, John Boehner, and other RINOS to accept 100% of the Obama Agenda as if it were ours. No Way!

McConnell and Boehner made promise after promise to we the people and kept none. Donald Trump brought in all the people who were fed up with Boehner and McConnell and who believed that the US was theirs, not the purview of a group of elitist legislators who had duped their constituency.

Others have felt similarly, and they have expressed their outrage in other ways than the ballot box. The fictitious Howard Beale might as well be real because he lit a candle under all who think sitting still is OK!

Howard Beale brings out the Trump in all of us

Yes, Howard Beale in the paragraphs below represents all of us frustrated Americans who seemingly have no chance because as Donald Trump would say, "The Game Is Rigged!" Beale's story, though unrelated to our national plight in 2016, still captures the mood and the emotions of Americans today regarding a government gone bad!

You may not remember Howard Beale because you are probably not old enough but many of you may have enough mileage to have seen the movie even if it were long after its debut in 1976.

So, if you have some baggage, and you have some time on your bones, you may remember back in November, 1976 when Howard Beale, as played by Peter Finch, the long-time anchor in the movie "Network News," gets the bad news that eventually causes him to utter one of the most famous movie lines of all time.

Beale gets fired and is given two weeks. The long-time anchor has a very poor reaction to this news and he cannot control himself during the next news broadcast.

He promises to commit suicide on the air. The company immediately fires him—no second chances for a repeat performance. No two weeks!

Beale is devastated and remorseful. He begs for the opportunity to say good-by to his fans with dignity, and he is given his last opportunity ever for air time so that he can say his good-by's, and also apologize on behalf of the network. Howard Beale gets his chance

Yet, once on the air, Beale sees the camera and understands the power of the camera, and he is overwhelmed by his continuing circumstance.

He goes into another diatribe starting off with a rant claiming that "Life is bullshit." He is so passionate that his ratings spike as he persuades his viewers to shout out of their windows: "I'm as mad as hell, and I'm not going to take this anymore!" That is the Howard Beale line heard 'round the world'.

"I'm as mad as hell, and I'm not going to take this anymore!" How many of voted for Trump Donald Trump with similar sentiments. "I'm as mad as hell, and I'm not going to take this anymore!"

Well, my fellow Americans, I bet you saw this coming, and I am going to deliver it as passionately in words as I can: "I am mad as hell, and I am not going to take this anymore." I bet you are too. Let me remind you of the "why" in all of this.

Taxes are too high; elected officials are out of touch; government is too big; spending is out of control; and the Affordable Healthcare Act (Obamacare) has become a train wreck, which President-elect Trump promises to correct.

As hard as it is to believe, American heroes, instead of getting well in government hospitals are dying in the VA system built with intentions to keep them well. Moreover, nobody, after spending $160 billion per year supposedly on Veterans' care, can tell us why our best patriots are being summarily neglected, and why they must wait years sometimes for appointments.

The people of America see the federal government as incompetent and corrupt. We Americans have no voice. Our last president exchanged five top Taliban Officers from Gitmo for one PFC, who we subsequently learned had abandoned his fellow troops and was declared a "traitor."

Additionally, and this is the worst: too many of US are too lazy to hold government accountable, and too many of our finest politicians are on the take.

I am writing this book about the Electoral College for you, a fellow American as frustrated as I, who wants to understand the system so that it can be made better. After you read this book, feel free to give the new President some tips. Your views on the Electoral College will be enhanced with sound logic simply by reading-on.

Government is presiding over a full-blown train wreck. Corporate leaches have infiltrated our government. We have record unemployment; illegal aliens are smiling as they take American jobs; an unsustainable status quo supports special interests over the people's interests and when we look to the future we see a public education system that should create our next heroes, we find that it creates mostly dummmies. The graduates are so dumb that they don't seem to mind being called dummmies. Scrooge would sum it up with a hearty: "Bah Humbug." It is that bad! Ask your neighbor!

We have the poorest economy since the depression with excessive welfare and income redistribution; institutionalized lying; a corrupt state-loving press that carries water for the Democratic Party. Before Trump, Democrats ran the national government without a care for the people.

We have a debt large enough to kill America by sapping all resources; huge student debt stopping graduates' success and an opportunity of a life and a family; tyranny v. democracy; government lawlessness; freedom and liberty in jeopardy; American stagnation, and a big loss of America's world prestige.

And, on top of that, the press beats its breast about its importance by suggesting that President Obama always learned about what was happening across the world by reading the newspapers; not by his daily security briefing. Nothing that happened in his eight years could be attributed (i.e. blamed) on him. Obama was coated with more Teflon than the Teflon Don, John Gotti. Nothing sticks to Obama. He is not to blame for anything.

Everybody in Washington but mostly the President got a free ride by the corrupt press with no accountability. It is that bad. America is not built for a dictator or an emperor. It is a Republic with a Constitution that governs everybody's behavior in favor of their country and all the people in the country (We the people).

Millenials have been brainwashed

The tender minds of our most recent adults are easily swayed. Our big government has become such a problem that most Americans believe that it can never again be the solution. The youth indoctrination in America for the last eight years begins in grade school. The Obama Department of Education is responsible. This is code for Obama is responsible but he won't take any blame. Our children sing propaganda songs praising the Democratic President.

Americans have been so beat down that there was little surprise that songs very much like those sung by Hitler Youth to achieve loyalty have been sung in US grade schools for years. We were all upset when we learned that our children were being taught to sing songs of praise to Barack Obama in the classroom at our local public school? Wouldn't you be upset?

Many of us have forgotten this as for eight years we had one outrage after another. Would you be outraged? Would you think that having school children sing songs of praise to Obama is more than a little creepy? Well, the truth is that it has been happening regularly. There are not just one or two isolated cases either.

Thanks to the Internet, you can see examples of brainwashed K-6 students with video of some of these songs. For me it is disgusting. Those who think Trump is an egotist forgot the master of ego, Barack Hussein Obama.

Because we think their brains are a little firmer than kids in grade school, we are outraged again but not quite so to learn that our future, the hope of America, our youth; even today go through colleges in huge numbers only to be unemployed and sacked with debt for life. They are trained by coffee-breath professors to accept their plight and not blame liberalism, progressivism, or Barack H. Obama, a millennial folk hero. I'll bet many of the parents of millennials voted for Trump for this reason alone.

Fresh graduates are given no hope. Yet, they too cast no blame on a president whose policies have caused their plight. They love this President, who is exiting so far gracefully, even though he did all he could to thwart their just efforts to be successful in life.

Worse than that, their coffee-breath professors in the colleges and universities filled their brains with garbage and they did their best to weaken their spirit. When you are out of spirit, help from a socialist government looks like a great alternative to nothing.

Coffee-breath professors teach the millennials to blame America, not themselves if they get a D or a C in an exam. Never blame the poor teaching of the coffee-breath professor. Likewise, never blame President Obama or his government for today's problems.

Of course, Obama and the Congress, but mostly Obama have created devastation for today's new graduates. There is no economy per se as when America was bustling with jobs. I dare you to find an open job that does not involve slipping something in between a bun, and manufacturing a sandwich.

When we cannot recognize a problem, it is all but impossible to solve it. Thankfully, there are some people like you, the readers of this book, who want to make America great again. And, we will. We began by electing Donald Trump though we have to fight the Electoral College and recount challenges

As a Democrat, I know that am smarter than most other Democrats. I know that the Democratic Party is the source of their ill fortune. Most Democrats deny this basic fact.

The Democratic Party has become a subversive organization, attempting to cause the decay of America from within. Yes, it has gotten that bad. As a Democrat, and a retired college professor, I can say that because I know that it is true. Americans, young and old, can do better than listening to the Democratic spew!

Millennials unfortunately have not been schooled well enough to think for themselves and so they do not believe that liberalism, progressivism, communism, and socialism are vile precepts for freedom loving people.

Thus, many young minds of today, corrupted by coffee-breath professors who have a hard time qualifying for faculty status in the faculty lounge, are already poisoned and some cannot recover. Many of these young minds, therefore are not willing to fight the bad guys to help make America great again! Hopefully, by reading and listening to sources other than the 200% corrupt media, and the their demented faculties, the new young will see the light over time if they can pick up some stray wisdom.

The millennials on college campuses especially, who need safe zones and free-speech zones to function, are too willing to fight against the good guys—yes, the good guys instead of those making their lives miserable. Instead, these folks, who God has blessed by placing them in the on-deck circle for success, have been taught to have disdain for success. Consequently, they pay tribute to the Soros collectors, and the *nothing matters but us groups* who care nothing about America.

The new millennial, who never had to make a decision in her life, will take you on—while they condone rioters and rabble rousers who want to take away the rudiments and fundamental liberties of other Americans. They do not get it and wherever they turn, there is another Facebook Friend who agrees that America is the problem.

America is not the problem. A great America is the solution.

Don't you wonder if these people really care about the Electoral College at all. Is this just a ruse--power play to delegitimatize Donald Trump or to place obstacles to his prospects for early success. Perhaps it is just an excuse to be able to enjoy a coffee with a liberal coffee-breath Democrat professor right outside the faculty lounge. Maybe?

This group of youngins, so vulnerable and yet so willing to have their minds captured are collectively known as millennials, and they love the notion of group-think. Yet, if their great minds were permitted to run on their own, this group could offer the best craniums the world has ever seen. Yet, their deficient faculty have coached them to not consider using their great brains to think through politics and other matters in life with open minds. And so, they wallow, and they blame America and other Americans for their misery. Their blame is misplaced but nobody can convince them they are wrong. They know it all.

The millennials will not admit it but they are the stupidest offspring America has ever produced in terms of their gullibility and their personal willingness to sacrifice their future for a promising promise from a half-wit coffee-breath professor. They are literally a new kind of stupid.

They should know better but they have no fortitude and persistence to work for anything good. Democrats know the great promises of the century. It takes a great mind to see them as they are. Millennials are pawns in a scheme they do not even understand.

Rush Limbaugh nets this notion out succinctly below:

"Donald Trump's gonna have perhaps the most embattled presidency in -- well, certainly in our lifetimes, and I dare say maybe in modern American history. They're not going to quit and they are a new kind of stupid. They are not logical. They make no sense whatsoever. But they are going to have the media on their side, and that's the danger."

"The media is going to make them look normal. The media is going to make these people look like they are the majority. The media is going to try to convince you that somehow something went wrong and that you are the real minority in this country and you didn't deserve to have this election win on your side. It's all an outrage. This is all they know in terms of how to behave and how to position things."

As a sexagenarian, and a professor for over thirty years in colleges and universities, I know what I have seen and so I know what I am talking about. I have no compunction to offer conclusions about my observations and analysis of millennials. They simply have no clue what life is about, and their minds are so numb that they do not even care about what they are missing.

I have seen them, in their supposed "innocence" protesting American heroes such as Condoleezza Rice and Dr. Ben Carson. Why, because they are black or because coffee-breath communist professors told them it was the right thing to do? It was the right way to greet people with whom their views conflict. For the naturally intolerant progressive left, being nasty to others is a given.

Both came to visit universities and were disrespected by the students, who unquestionably were lame brain, affected by the coffee-breath faculty—avowed liberal progressive socialists.

Rutgers for example in 2013 picked a boardwalk babe, Snooki, rather than an American who loves America to give them their final address at their university. Hope is reserved for people who have never met today's millennials.

Students are guided by communist professors in universities and the students now accept that communism is OK. These are the elite progressive professors in their universities who believe free speech cannot be tolerated and who fill the heads of the millennials with mush—especially intolerance for new thought and logical thought.

Their importance is endorsed by the universities when they get to be all gussied up in their finest plumage and adornments at commencement ceremonies, and they process before all others to the graduation stage. With such guidance, students have learned that they really do know it all, though their parents have no clue what happened to them on campus. Parents cannot recognize their children when they come home for breaks.

The administrators and the progressive / communist faculty and student lemmings at a once respected university named Rutgers, embarrassed conservative speakers including a fine American, Dr. Condoleezza Rice. Rice was scheduled to be commencement speaker. She is a major US historical figure besides being an academic in her own right.

The students, faculty, and administration were nasty and unwelcoming to her and they protested her choice as commencement speaker. Rice appropriately rescinded her acceptance. The children have taken over the asylum and they are being guided by the communist coffee-breath quasi-intellectuals. Parents need to understand what is happening on campuses across the nation.

Students who are not rich are overwhelmed upon graduation with a huge loan burden equaling that of a home mortgage. No wonder they cannot buy homes. For all their achievements in college, their faculty are still employed, and they are not. Their campus lives are over. Time to go home to mom and dad.

The student loan burden prevents former student borrowers from buying homes, cars, and having a family. Yet students do not blame their elite coffee-breath faculty and their establishment universities or the President who created their dilemma—for anything.

They blame George Bush for everything still because some talk show host once told them that works for him. It is great to have brains today; it is just not respected if one decides to use them for the public good.

Only retirees in their 90's can afford honeymoon cottages while looking for their next spouse. As many as 37 million student loan borrowers are too broke to engage in basic life. College loans, instead of lifting people to the top, have created a new race to the bottom,

On the International stage, America's popular President presents people like those reading this book as bad actors. The recent Democratic candidate referred to us all as deplorables. Frustrated zealots from the left are making sure nobody gives America a break on the world platform. The US government now seems to want to make the rest of the world strong by making America weak.

The weaknesses of America are magnified by a corrupt press because Americans have been doing too well for too long. A lot more than a few illegal foreign interlopers have helped the progressives diminish America's good fortune. The demagogues would have Americans believe their failing to get a job is due to white privilege or for something stupid like being an American too long.

None of this helps command respect for our country from anybody but the white guilt-ridden university students and their "lucky to have a job" mentors on the faculty. Having been a faculty member, I know how bad things are.

The only people who seem to care have names like John Q. Public and John Doe. Thank you to both Johns for choosing this book about America, the Constitution, and the Electoral College.

Nobody in the world gives America a standing ovation anymore. Nobody asks us for curtain calls. Our leaders turn their backs on our friends and seem to pay homage to our enemies. How is this? Has Congress lost all its power? Who has the power in the US? The Constitution says it is the people!

Smaller and weaker countries such as Russia, Iran, and North Korea continue to push US around and laugh at US, and our only response is to see if somehow it might have been because we may have offended them. And the top issue of the day is not how to save the country, it's "Why is there an Electoral College?"

We show our greatness by counting the number of hits on a *hashtag of **bring our girls home,*** when no Americans are missing, and we expect terrorists to cower when the number of twitter resends hits a million.

We also refuse to have an honest discussion about why four Americans, including the US Ambassador, were permitted to die in Benghazi when the military says they were prepared to save them. The then Secretary of State responsible for their deaths is then able to run for president as if their deaths do not matter.

We have had an administration that blames the Christian Government of Nigeria for not reaching out enough to the Muslim killers who kidnapped 300 girls as sex slaves. Boko Haram had captured and killed 49 boys just a few weeks before this particular outrage. When will they ever learn?

The captors boldly announced they would sell them on the sex slave market, and the US is powerless in its feeble response. The new strategy is to permit time to go by so those who are at fault can claim that it is old news.

What has happened to our good sense? Should there not be a set of laws written by sane people so that insane acts cannot occur without retribution?

Why do our representatives, especially Republicans who have lots of heart choose not to represent America? Republican elites in the establishment pretended to be Democrats until Donald Trump came along.

For me, these have been the worst days of America that I have ever witnessed. Yet, our government seems to have no problems that are in need of solutions. Clear-thinking Americans look at today's leaders as hapless, without the wherewithal to tie their own shoes. We expect a lot from the President-elect.

We have yearned for a guy like Donald Trump to come forth to save us. These leaders tried to force all Americans to be happy in a state of mediocrity, rather than by being outstanding. "Don't worry: Be Happy!" Now that Donald Trump has been selected by the agreed-on method, the Electoral College, the new experts want us to believe his election was not legitimate.

If you have been paying attention, and I sure hope you have been--as it is a civic duty—you know that there are even more issues than the exhaustive list we just walked you through. Isn't that a shame on US—especially our inept leadership and of course us for tolerating their buffoonish acts and elite selfishness.

I think that as much as the Electoral College is a new perplexity, the exhaustive list of issues is a big reason that you bought this book. Thank you very much.

The Constitution of which the Electoral College is a part, is a survivor's guide to dealing with a corrupt nation; a corrupt press; a corrupt government and corrupt politicians who believe they can trick us all into finding them acceptable.

The Founders wrote the Constitution not to solve an America gone bad but to prevent America from going bad. Yet, corrupt politicians have taken us to the precipice. There is no time like today to make America great again.

Since you chose to buy this book, I know you and I are on the right side and thankfully we are on the same side. Together, we can all help arrest control of our government back from perpetrators wishing to destroy US.

We first must understand what is going on and we then must understand our rights. Books such as this as well as other Brian W. Kelly books such as *America 4 Dummmies*; *The Constitution 4 Dummmies*; and *The Bill of Rights 4 Dummmies,* are well-needed to combat the gospel as spouted by the corrupt media.

Even before you and I and everybody else are on board, just like Howard Beale, we must start the first wave of solutions by opening our windows all the way and shouting as loud as we all can: "I am mad as hell, and I am not going to take this anymore."

Then, we must make sure that we talk to all of the other "dummmies" out there that we know—people like you and I and others, and let's help them know that unless we all fully engage in America, when we wake up from our deep fog, there may be no America left for our progeny. We will have blown it for sure if we choose to permit by action or inaction this travesty to happen. We are very close to losing our country.

Chapter 4 Back to History For Some Good Answers

When we think of the Electoral College and the Founders, would these be fair questions: "**1**. Is it possible that the Founders were just simpletons who cared only about their own businesses?" "**2**. Could it have been that these highly successful merchants put together a group of inquisitors and enforcers to assure the success of US commercial interests, such as theirs, in America at its founding.

"**3**. Has anybody asked why such top level American big shots would care one iota about the common man? Would it be un-common?" "**4**. Can it have to do with goodness and God?" "**5**. Did such men and women exist at the founding and if so do such men exist still today?"

Please know that I have great respect for the Founders, the Revolution, and the Constitution. I ask you to excuse my crassness in the above questioning of the Founders' motivations.

Unexceptional normal human beings might be more concerned about their own businesses than business and commerce in general. If given enforcement power, much like today's "innocently" corrupt American officials, today's politicos would be more prone to enforce that which helps their own standing, rather than that of their fellow man.

And, yes, the Founders were important men but they were exceptional men in their times. They cared about goodness and the cared earnestly about people. They simply were not normal run of the mill human beings. They were special and they came together just at the right time for America.

It is good for Americans to ponder the motivations of the Founders. This gives us all a clearer understanding of why those brave men who came before us risked their blood, treasure and sacred honor to create the greatest nation on Earth.

Maybe they were sent by God.

The Founding Fathers were a revolutionary group, diverse in their professions and yet unified in their goal: American liberty. Of course, not just the common man would receive liberty in the end but the Founders also had been subject to the tyranny of the British, and they too longed to be free.

They understood that not just the leaders but also the citizens should have a say in their government and that a government only derives its legitimate power from the consent of the governed.

When Thomas Jefferson wrote the Declaration of Independence, his timeless, eloquent words of freedom sent political shock waves around the world that continue to reverberate in the minds of revolutionaries everywhere. These are the words of a God-fearing man:

"We hold these truths to be self-evident, that all men are created equal, that they are endowed by their Creator with certain unalienable Rights, that among these are Life, Liberty and the pursuit of Happiness. — That to secure these rights, Governments are instituted among Men, deriving their just powers from the consent of the governed, — That whenever any Form of Government becomes destructive of these ends, it is the Right of the People to alter or to abolish it, and to institute new Government, laying its foundation on such principles and organizing its powers in such form, as to them shall seem most likely to effect their Safety and Happiness."

Most of the Founders were god-fearing men. However, some notable exceptions included Thomas Paine and Ethan Allen. They may have even been hostile to evangelical Christianity. However, they were provocative agents of the Revolution. Men like Paine and Allen were not intellectual architects of the Constitution but they believed in America. Thomas Paine for example, did not arrive in this country until 1774 and he only stayed a short time.

Looking at the normal list of Founders and patriots, we would find others, such as George Washington, Patrick Henry, Samuel Adams, John Jay, James Madison, John Witherspoon, Alexander Hamilton, John Adams, and even Thomas Jefferson. These men were influenced by goodness and by God.

Their formal writings, including their personal correspondence, biographies, and public statements, are loaded with salient quotations showing that these thinkers had political philosophies deeply influenced by Christianity.

It is this lesser known aspect of the Constitution that is the focus of this chapter. Jefferson often spoke of the purpose of the Constitution as a means by which to "fortify us against the degeneracy of one government, and the concentration of all its powers in the hands of the one, the few, the well-born, or the many." He assumed that informed citizens could and would make good decisions for themselves and their country.

"I have so much confidence in the good sense of man, and his qualifications for self-government, that I am never afraid of the issue where reason is left free to exert her force."

What did Jefferson mean by "one" government? He meant a government in which power was not divided. It was a government concentrated in one body, one group, or one person. Jefferson believed in government of the people, for the people, and by the people.

Jefferson, a farmer by trade, but clearly an able intellectual and eloquent statesman, had great faith in the goodness and wisdom of people who worked the soil – farmers and planters like himself. "State a problem to a ploughman and a professor," he said, and "the former will decide it often better than the latter."

He would find many more reasons to believe this if he were to interview today's coffee-breath professors at American universities. Jefferson worried about a government with too much power. He was OK with a government lacking power. He believed the power should be vested in the people.

Adams expounded on this idea:

"No simple form of government can possibly secure men against the violence of power. … Monarchy [turns into] despotism, aristocracy [into] oligarchy, and democracy will soon degenerate into an anarchy, such an anarchy that every man will do what is right in his own eyes [an allusion to Judges 21:25], and no man's life or property or reputation or liberty will be secure and every one of these will soon mold itself into a system of subordination of all the moral virtues and intellectual abilities, all the powers of wealth, beauty, wit, and science, to the wanton pleasures, the capricious will, and the execrable cruelty of one or a very few." Amen!

These are a part of the background thought for why we are a constitutional Republic, and not a pure democracy. The Constitution is a guiding light from which our elected leaders are not permitted to stray. For a better look at the Constitution, I unabashedly recommend my book, *The Constitution 4 Dummmies* available on Amazon and Kindle.

As we look at the Founders and the Constitution, remember again that the Electoral College is a fundamental principle defined in the Constitution by the Founders.

Chapter 5 The Founding of the Electoral College

Founders concerned about the common man

The Founders who attended the Constitutional Convention in Philadelphia devised the Electoral College as a fair way to determine how the president of the United States would be elected. They were not demented as many Democrats today would have you believe. They were very concerned about the common man?

One thing is for sure, there were no Democrats or Republicans or Greens or Libertarians or any political Parties permitted in America at the time of the first presidents. The founders were profoundly unselfish beings looking after the good of America and their fellow man. Though they had their own mercantile interests; they were altruistic in their work for America. The more we read about the Founders, and the more we see the risks they took for a just moral cause, the more we can safely suggest they were good men.

The Constitutional Convention

The Convention met between May and September of 1787 to address the problems of the weak central government that was the hallmark of the Articles of Confederation. The Arricles of Confederation may have initially formed the "Union." However, it was not as perfect as a definition of government asit could be. Thus, when the Constitution was built, in the preamble, its purpose was form a "more perfect union."

The United States Constitution emerged from this convention. It established a federal government with more specific powers, than the "Articles," including those related to conducting relations with foreign governments.

The form of government was called a Constitutional Republic. The constitutional part meant that relied on a Constitution (A written set of rules), not the whim of the leadership. The Republic part means that the people as individuals hold the power—not the government or the governed as a group. The US therefore is technically not a democracy. Minority interests are part and parcel of the Constitution.

Let's first look at some thoughts on a Republic.

It is that form of government in which the powers of sovereignty are vested in the people and are exercised by the people, either directly, or through representatives chosen by the people, to whom those powers are specially delegated.

The word "people" as used above may be either plural or singular. In a Republic, the group only has advisory powers; the sovereign individual is free to reject the majority group-think. The USA does have one exception to this: if 100% of a jury convicts, then the individual loses sovereignty and is subject to group-think as in a democracy.

Let's now look at some thoughts on a Democracy.

It is that form of government in which the sovereign power resides in and is exercised by the whole body of free citizens as a group, directly or indirectly through a system of representation, as distinguished from a monarchy, aristocracy, or oligarchy.

It is worthy of note that in a pure democracy, 51% beats 49%. In other words, the minority has no rights. The minority only has those privileges granted specifically by the dictatorship of the majority.

Let's look at a simple way to contrast a Republic with a democracy.

A Republic and a democracy are identical in every aspect except one. In a Republic, the sovereignty is in each individual person. In a Democracy, the sovereignty is in the group. In a Republic therefore, the minority side has rights. In a democracy, only the majority side has rights.

The Improved Federal System v the Articles

Under the reformed federal system, many of the responsibilities for foreign affairs fell under the authority of an executive branch, as defined within the Constitution.

There were however, important powers, such as treaty ratification that remained the responsibility of the legislative branch.

When the necessary number of state ratifications took place, the Constitution became the official written definition of the United States Government. It came into effect in 1789 and has served as the basis of the United States Government ever since. It has been modified 27 times via twenty-seven separately ratified Amendments.

Are the people as a whole smart enough to directly elect a president?

Many Constitutional expert sources attest that the Framers were wary of giving the people the power to directly elect the President — some felt the citizenry would be too beholden to local interests, and too easily duped by promises or shenanigans. Another argument against the popular vote was that in a national election, in a time of oil lamps and quill pens, it was just impractical to get votes from every person.

There were lots of proposals as there were lots of smart people thinking about the best and fairest way to select a US president. Some would have given the power to the Congress, but this did not sit well with those who wanted to see true separation of the branches of the new government.

Others felt it would be OK if the state legislatures decided. After all, state representatives are elected by the people. Opponents of using state representatives thought this would make the new president too beholden to state interests. The Electoral College, was proposed by James Wilson. It was the compromise that the Constitutional Convention reached. When you take the time to understand it, it makes a lot of sense.

Proportional representation just like the US House

Though it was not exactly easy to figure out when Wilson proposed it, the Electoral College has evolved into something whose proportional representation numbers are reasonably easy to understand. Each state receives a number of votes in the Electoral College equal to its total representation in both Houses of Congress.

Let's look at a few examples to get this notion down solid: California, which has 53 representatives in the US House of Representatives based on its population and two in the Senate, casts 55 votes in the Electoral College. Pennsylvania, which has 18 representatives in the House and two in the Senate, casts 20 votes in the Electoral College. Rhode Island, which has 2 representatives in the House and two in the Senate, casts 4 votes in the Electoral College.

The big exception to the number of electoral votes is Washington D.C. The District of Columbia has one representative in the House. The House Representative has no vote. There are no senators elected from Washington DC.

By a Constitutional Amendment # 23, ratified by the states, Washington, D.C., was given three electoral votes for president. Until the 23rd Amendment of the United States Constitution was ratified in 1961, Washington, D.C., residents did not have the right to vote in presidential elections, being governed, as per the Constitution, solely by Congress.

If there were not so much concern from the Founders of collusion among big shots in government in the formation of informal "big shot" "hoity toity" elite establishment clubs, the most logical choice would be for those duly elected by the people in each state to the State House and the State Senate to also default to be the electors for that state.

Another easy allocation method would have been to not have electors and thus have no vote at all. In this scenario, the apportioned number such as 55 for California, 20 for Pennsylvania, 4 for Rhode Island, and 3 for Washington DC would be used. They could simply be added up.

This would make it easier as electors would not have to be "elected" and there would not have to be an election of the president by electors. The apportioned total would count as a ballot cast for the state winner. The total votes for all state electors would determine who would be President.

The Founders wanted the electors to be people rather than a direct number as it gave the Republic one last opportunity to stop a scoundrel from becoming president. Let's say that some good cause was determined and it was universally accepted that the high electoral vote achiever was a thief or scoundrel or both and other obvious proven-true bad things.

When the electors would meet (In 2016, the date was December 19), they could vote a different person than who the people in their states selected. However, other than when there is a major obvious issue of detrimental circumstance to the country, electors are sworn to vote for the winner of the state.

There is more to it.

Each formal US census, conducted by law every ten years, determines how many representatives each state gets. Thus, it follows that after each census, the number of electors in the Electoral College for each state is also recalculated. Therefore, when the general election is held, the people of California decide what to do with their 55 electoral votes. In other words, they select their electors according to their own rules; not the rules of a central government. Every other state makes like decisions.

Let's move to the current presidential election now for more realism. In this past election since majority wins, the State of California decided to give its 55 votes to Hillary Clinton. Should the Trump people have complained about the potential for fraud in such a large majority.

There are reasons why the popular vote is a bad idea? First, it is because our form of government is Republic, not democracy and so, the minority has a voice, not just the majority.

Here is another reason. Let's say everybody from California could make it to the polls and they all voted for candidate X. Candidate X would receive about 18 million popular votes and 55 electoral votes. Now, in the other forty-nine states, suppose the polls were not open long enough for all voters to vote and so, let's say only 100 were able to vote and they all voted for candidate Y.   Forty nine states times 100 equals 49,000.

Thus the popular vote would be 38 million v 49,000 and candidate X would win a landslide victory over candidate Y. Is this fair when the total population of the states that could not vote in this scenario is 241,000,000 minus California (38,000,000). So, the 38 million California residents would preempt the 203 million other US residents.

If you are from California in this scenario, you are happy. If you are from any of the other 49 states, your state's population along with all the other states of 203,000,000 gets beaten by just one state with just 38,000,000 in population.

So, what the Founders did was took every state's total population and even if only one person in that state votes or just 100 people vote, their voter population determines how much their state is worth in terms of determining the president.

So, let's say there are no electors. Instead, the population in each state is the determinant. The popular vote equivalent of the Electoral College would be that if 1 person votes in California, all 38 million registered population adds to the count for candidate A. If 1 person in Pennsylvania votes, all 9 million registered population add to the count for candidate B. If 1 person in Michigan votes, all 7 million registered population add to the count for candidate B. If 1 person in Florida votes, all 13 million population add to the count for candidate B.

If there were just these four states, Candidate A would win 38,000,000 v 29,000,000

Now if we make it 5 states and we add Texas' number of 15 million registered for candidate B, then B wins by 44,000,000 to 38,000,000

This system protects the viability of all states and weighs them equally regardless of whether the registered voters in the state cast a ballot or not.

The Electoral College works almost exactly like this except for one thing. It proportionally reduces these large numbers to manageable numbers. Its logic is the same, however. It does not penalize states that have low voter turnout whether they vote Democrat or Republican or other. Almost every state uses the winner takes all method so this description of the fairness of proportionality voting based on states' populations holds true.

Only two states, Nebraska and Maine, do not follow the winner-takes-all rule. In Maine, each Party's state convention nominates four electors, one from each congressional district and two at large. In Nebraska, there are three congressional districts, meaning two votes go to a statewide winner and the three districts each award one electoral vote.

The total population of the US is thus divided up by state so that there is a total of 538 electors in the "Electoral College." It works the same way proportionally as if the big numbers such as 38 million for California and 15 million for Texas were used.

A majority of 270 electoral votes is required to elect the President. Your state's entitled allotment of electors equals the number of members in its Congressional delegation: one for each member in the House of Representatives plus two for your two Senators.

What really happened in California in 2016?

On the day we took our sample, Hillary Clinton had already received 7,362,490 votes. Donald Trump had received 3,916,209. Gary Johnson and Jill Stein received an inconsequential number of electoral ballots. So we won't even count them.

Hillary Clinton whooped Donald Trump by about 3.5 million votes. They say there are still over 3 million ballots to count in California. The margin of victory in this state is not inconsequential. Many Americans in the rest of the states do not like the idea that California, which has a huge illegal foreign national population, would be the determining state for the presidency of the country. For the other 49, with Governor Jerry Brown telling residents legal and illegal to vote, there are a lot of suspicions.

In fact, because of California, those who suggest the Electoral College is all claptrap must be OK with letting California determine who the President of the US should be. The count when this was written placed Hillary Clinton ahead by 2 million in the popular vote. Simply because she and Donald Trump decided to abide by the Constitution, her supporters say she is not President-elect.

Let's look at the agreed upon method to determine the World Series. In the 2016 World Series, The Chicago Cubs pulled off a thrilling win in 10 innings over the Cleveland Indians to end their 108-year World Series title drought. The Series was tied three games to three. To Hillary supporters, however, the Indians were ahead 20 to 19 because the Indians had scored twenty-runs in six games to nineteen runs for the Cubs.

The final game was won 8 to 7 by the Cubs making the run total equal at 27. Yet the World Series was awarded to the Cubs because they had won seven games. The run total did not matter. Only the agreed upon method of games won mattered. The same goes for the 2016 presidential election. The popular vote total did not matter. Only the agreed upon method of electoral votes mattered.

Victories and losses in all endeavors are determined according to the rules and the rules do not get changed after the games or the series of games are played. The Cleveland Indians Fans, if they used Hillary supporter logic, would have been asking for a tie-breaker game to see who would win the World Series on the highest total runs. Of course there is one big problem with that logic. The teams had agreed and the rules were thus set that the winner of the best of seven series would win the World Series. And, so the Cubs ended their 108-year drought and were declared the victors according to the rules of engagement.

Let's use one more analogy. Just suppose West Virginia was one of our largest states and they came in proportionately favoring Donald Trump. Remember Donald Trump was not in favor of extinguishing the coal fires across the nation. Trump wanted West Virginians to be able to have high paying coal jobs. This would be the same as California favoring Hillary Clinton because she believes lawless immigration should be made the law of the land.

Using the West Virginia actual numbers times one hundred, what if the Trump numbers X (times) 100 came in at 48,619,800? What if the Hillary numbers came in at 18,745,700? These are in fact the exact WV proportions.

This would mean that approximately 30 million additional voters would have voted for Trump in West Virginia. If Trump lost the election in the Electoral College, and won the popular vote because of his huge majority in West Virginia, would this be a good enough reason to let West Virginia determine the presidency?

Should Trump in such a circumstance in which he won the popular vote but not the electoral vote, be declared President-elect even though it was against the rules. Or should Hillary be given the victory since her tally was within the rules?

If it is not a good reason for West Virginia in the hypothetical, then it is not a good reason for California in the actual realm. The 3.5 million majority in California is not a good enough reason to permit California to determine exclusively the presidency of the United States of America. That's why the popular vote is not used.

By the way, the population of California is moving out. The state population is thus declining. People are moving to other states. Many are heading out to Texas, which is much more business friendly and the Texas economy is doing very well and taxes are low.

So, a high population state one day might be substantially lower in population thirty years or so down the road. The population of Texas is expected to double by 2050, says a new report released by the Office of the State Demographer. I suspect that Californians would not want Texas to be the determining factor in determining national elections.

If you are still not sure that this system is fair, please read the email at the end of chapter 1, one more time.

Who created the states

Please check out the name of our country. Our full name is the United States of America. It is not the Solitary or Individual States of America. Each of the states has its own local government and it is these local governments called states that together form the country we love.

The colonies already had defined the geographies of the 13 original states. The national government did not create the states. We are not the result of a proportioned federal government in which various geographical pieces have been randomly broken off the full country into geographical shares. Each state instead, is a sovereign entity. However, by agreeing to the Constitution, each state also became a part of a union of states which formed the national government.

How do electors get selected for the Electoral College?

We already know how many votes each state gets in the Electoral College. None of this really matters if those electoral votes are not cast. But, by whom?

On Election Day, it is the voters in each state who select their state's Electors by simply casting their ballots for President. Who are the electors by name?

People in the states who vote for the president are not typically tuned in to the fact that their state legislature or perhaps another official state body, has already selected which people in the state will serve as the actual electors.

There is no separate vote by the people for the electors. When the electors vote (In 2016, the date is December 19), in 50 separate elections in 50 states, they pledge to vote for the candidate that the people in their state have selected in the general election.

Depending on the laws of each state; they may be state elected officials, state Party leaders, or people in the state who have a personal or political affiliation with their Party's presidential candidate. They pledge, based on a major penalty to vote for the candidate in the Electoral College who won the state's electoral votes. If they go rogue, there are unpleasant consequences

Chapter 6   The Constitutional Convention Considered Multiple Electoral Options

More ways than one to skin a cat

The delegates at the Constitutional Convention (May to September 1787) considered several possible methods for selecting a president. Let's look at these now more formally than in Chapter 5. Then, we will show the end result of their work as reflected within the Constitution itself.

Idea One at the convention was to have the US Congress, a body duly elected by the people of the states to choose the president. This idea was rejected.

Some felt that making such a choice would be too divisive an issue and leave too many hard feelings in the Congress. Others felt that such a procedure would invite unseemly political bargaining, corruption, and perhaps even interference from foreign powers. Still others felt that such an arrangement would upset the balance of power between the legislative and executive branches of the federal government. In essence, idea 1 would permit the Congress to determine the Executive Branch.

Idea Two was to have the State lawmakers select the president. This idea was also rejected.

There were fears that a president would be so beholden to the state legislatures that it might permit them to erode federal authority and thus undermine the whole idea of a federation of states.

Idea Three was to have the president elected by a direct popular vote. Just count the votes. The Hillary Clinton campaign along with major donors, who watched her popular vote total grow to over two million more than Donald Trump's numbers began to espouse this notion in November 2016.

There are two reasons in 2016 for this to have happened.

1. There was a remote possibility that the supporters could create a groundswell of support for the idea and be able to do something before the new administration was finalized in the Electoral College.

2. They would be able to plant the seeds of doubt into the minds of Americans in an attempt to delegitimize the Trump Presidency, making it easier for a Democrat to win next time out.

The Founders rejected idea 3, known as direct election. The reason was not that the Framers of the Constitution doubted public intelligence but rather because they feared that without sufficient information about candidates from outside their own state, people would naturally vote for a "favorite son," from their own state or region.

It helps to remember that there were no political Parties when the country was formed and therefore there was no primary election to make the candidate pool manageable.

At worst in this scenario, no president would emerge with a popular majority sufficient to govern the whole country. At best, the choice of president would always be decided by the largest, most populous States with little regard for the smaller ones.

An **Idea Four** was also examined. With this, a so-called "Committee of Eleven" in the Constitutional Convention proposed an indirect election of the president through a College of Electors.

The description of how this would work, considering there were no political Parties is as follows: The function of the College of Electors in choosing the president could be likened to that in the Roman Catholic Church when the College of Cardinals select a new Pope.

The Electoral College original idea was for the most knowledgeable and informed individuals from each State to select the president based solely on merit and without regard to state of origin or political Party.

Looking back at its original structure, the Electoral College can be traced to the Centurial Assembly system of the Roman Republic. Under that system, the adult male citizens of Rome were divided, according to their wealth, into groups of 100 (aptly called Centuries).

Each group of 100 was entitled to cast only one vote either in favor or against proposals submitted to them by the Roman Senate. In the Electoral College system, the original 13 States serve as the Centurial groups (though they are not, of course, based on wealth). The number of votes per state would be determined by the size of each State's Congressional delegation. Still, the two systems are similar in design and share many of the same advantages and disadvantages.

The similarities between the Electoral College and classical institutions are not accidental. Many of the Founding Fathers were well schooled in historical matters including ancient history, ancient governments and their lessons.

The Constitution defines the Electoral College

Article I Section I of the Constitution defines the Legislative Branch as follows:

*All legislative powers herein granted shall be vested in a Congress of the **United States**, which shall consist of a Senate and House of Representatives.*

The notion of the Electoral college when put to paper appeared in Article II of the US Constitution. The Founders and others of their day wrote in a style that is less easy to read. Many comfortable with the prose style of today would not find the 18th century style appropriate prose today. So, when reading the Constitution, you may have to read again and again to get the exact gist. Article II reads exactly as follows:

Article. II. Executive Power

Section 1.
The executive Power shall be vested in a President of the United States of America. He shall hold his Office during the Term of four Years, and, together with the Vice President, chosen for the same Term, be elected, as follows:

Each State shall appoint, in such Manner as the Legislature thereof may direct, a Number of Electors, equal to the whole Number of Senators and Representatives to which the State may be entitled in the Congress: but no Senator or Representative, or Person holding an Office of Trust or Profit under the United States, shall be appointed an Elector.

The Electors shall meet in their respective States, and vote by Ballot for two Persons, of whom one at least shall not be an Inhabitant of the same State with themselves. And they shall make a List of all the Persons voted for, and of the Number of Votes for each; which List they shall sign and certify, and transmit sealed to the Seat of the Government of the United States, directed to the President of the Senate. The

President of the Senate shall, in the Presence of the Senate and House of Representatives, open all the Certificates, and the Votes shall then be counted.

The Person having the greatest Number of Votes shall be the President, if such Number be a Majority of the whole Number of Electors appointed; and if there be more than one who have such Majority, and have an equal Number of Votes, then the House of Representatives shall immediately chuse [choose] by Ballot one of them for President; and if no Person have a Majority, then from the five highest on the List the said House shall in like Manner choose the President.

But in choosing the President, the Votes shall be taken by States, the Representation from each State having one Vote; A quorum for this purpose shall consist of a Member or Members from two thirds of the States, and a Majority of all the States shall be necessary to a Choice. In every Case, after the Choice of the President, the Person having the greatest Number of Votes of the Electors shall be the Vice President. But if there should remain two or more who have equal Votes, the Senate shall choose from them by Ballot the Vice President.

The Congress may determine the Time of choosing the Electors, and the Day on which they shall give their Votes; which Day shall be the same throughout the United States.

No Person except a natural born Citizen, or a Citizen of the United States, at the time of the Adoption of this Constitution, shall be eligible to the Office of President; neither shall any Person be eligible to that Office who shall not have attained to the Age of thirty-five Years, and been fourteen Years a Resident within the United States.

In Case of the Removal of the President from Office, or of his Death, Resignation, or Inability to discharge the Powers and Duties of the said Office, the Same shall devolve on the Vice President, and the Congress may by Law provide for the Case of Removal, Death, Resignation or Inability, both of the President and Vice President, declaring what Officer shall then act as President, and such Officer shall act accordingly, until the Disability be removed, or a President shall be elected.

The President shall, at stated Times, receive for his Services, a Compensation, which shall neither be increased nor diminished during the Period for which he shall have been elected, and he shall not receive within that Period any other Emolument from the United States, or any of them.

Before he enter on the Execution of his Office, he shall take the following Oath or Affirmation:--"I do solemnly swear (or affirm) that I will faithfully execute the Office of President of the United States, and will to the best of my Ability, preserve, protect and defend the Constitution of the United States."

[Explanation of Article II Section I:

The purpose of Article II is to establish the second of the three branches of government, the Executive Branch. The Legislative Branch (House & Senate) is defined in Article I.

Article II Section 1 establishes the office of the President and the Vice-President. It sets their terms to be four years for each of them.

Presidents are not elected by the people per se. Instead, there is this notion called the Electoral College, and they elect the President. The people have a big say in the matter as they vote for Electoral College delegates who then vote for the President per their state's laws.

Each state has one vote in the "Electoral College" for each member of Congress. By voting for a candidate, the people are in effect voting for electors who will vote for that candidate. There are typically no separate elections for electors.

Originally, the President was the person with the most votes and the Vice-President was the person with the second most, though this was later changed to recognize that a Democrat

President should have a Democrat Vice President and a Republican President should have a Republican Vice president.

This was not always the case. Once political Parties were permitted, the 12th Amendment assured that the President and Vice President would always be of the same political Party.

By 1792, opposition to the policies of the Federalist Party was growing. Led by Secretary of State Thomas Jefferson (1743– 1826), critics of the Federalists banded together to form the Republican Party. They were also called Democratic-Republicans or Jeffersonian Republicans. It is not the same Republican Party from which Abraham Lincoln was elected President.

The election of 1796 was the first in which voters could choose between competing political Parties. It was also the first test of whether the nation could transfer power through a contested election.

The Federalists chose Vice President John Adams as their presidential candidate, and the Republicans, aka Democratic-Republicans selected Thomas Jefferson.
When John Adams became President, he was a member of the now long-gone Federalist Party. He was running against other Federalists as well as Democratic Republicans.

Under the electoral system at the time, each presidential elector was to vote twice, with the candidate who received the most votes becoming president and the candidate who came in second becoming vice president. Thomas Pinckney was a leading Federalist challenger to John Adams. There was no notion of a running mate.

The election was filled with shenanigans. Alexander Hamilton, for example, did not want John Adams as President. So, he convinced some southern electors to drop Adams's name from their ballots, while still voting for Pinckney. It was Hamilton's hope that Pinckney would receive more votes than Adams and be elected president.

When New Englanders learned of this plan, they dropped Pinckney from their ballots, ensuring that Adams won the election. When the final votes were tallied, Adams received 71 votes, only 3 more than Jefferson. As a result, Jefferson became vice president with 68 votes. . Pinckney was o-u-t. He had received fifty-nine elector votes

Aaron Burr, had been Jefferson's choice for VP. in the election of 1796.

Despite being from different Parties, Adams and Jefferson were thereby elected as the President and Vice-President respectively for four years. After Adams, the next highest vote getter was Thomas Jefferson.

Why did we need the 12ᵗʰ Amendment?

The twelfth Amendment was brought forth, passed and ratified by the states so that both the President and Vice-President heretofore would be from the same political Party even if it were the Rathskellar Party or the Liquor Party! There are other provisions including a clarification of the Electoral College.

In Article II, Section I, other minimum requirements were established, such as a 35-year minimum age. Presidents must also be natural-born citizens of the United States. The President is to be paid a salary, which cannot change, up or down, for the term in which he is in office.

The Twelfth Amendment to the United States Constitution outlines the necessary procedure for electing the President and Vice President. The Twelfth Amendment replaced Article II, Section 1, and Clause 3, which offered the original procedure by which the Electoral College was created and how it subsequently functioned.

Further clarification of the 12th Amendment: The 12th Amendment stipulates that members of the Electoral College will vote for President and Vice President separately. If no presidential candidate gets a majority of the electoral votes, the House picks the new president from the top 3 recipients of electoral votes. If no Vice-Presidential candidate gets a majority, the Senate picks the new VP from the top 2. The exact text of the 12th Amendment is contained below:

The 12th amendment

AMENDMENT XII of the Constitution of the United States of America

Passed by Congress December 9, 1803. Ratified June 15, 1804.

Note: A portion of Article II, section 1 of the Constitution was superseded by the 12th amendment.

The Electors shall meet in their respective states, and vote by ballot for President and Vice-President, one of whom, at least, shall not be an inhabitant of the same state with themselves; they shall name in their ballots the person voted for as President, and in distinct ballots the person voted for as Vice-President, and they shall make distinct lists of all persons voted for as President, and all persons voted for as Vice-President and of the number of votes for each, which lists they shall sign and certify, and transmit sealed to the seat of the government of the United States, directed to the President of the Senate.

The President of the Senate shall, in the presence of the Senate and House of Representatives, open all the certificates and the votes shall then be counted.

The person having the greatest Number of votes for President, shall be the President, if such number be a majority of the whole number of Electors appointed; and if no person have such majority, then from the

persons having the highest numbers not exceeding three on the list of those voted for as President, the House of Representatives shall choose immediately, by ballot, the President. But in choosing the President, the votes shall be taken by states, the representation from each state having one vote; a quorum for this purpose shall consist of a member or members from two-thirds of the states, and a majority of all the states shall be necessary to a choice. And if the House of Representatives shall not choose a President whenever the right of choice shall devolve upon them, before the fourth day of March next following, then the Vice-President shall act as President, as in the case of the death or other constitutional disability of the President.[Note 1]

The person having the greatest number of votes as Vice-President, shall be the Vice-President, if such number be a majority of the whole number of Electors appointed, and if no person have a majority, then from the two highest numbers on the list, the Senate shall choose the Vice-President; a quorum for the purpose shall consist of two-thirds of the whole number of Senators, and a majority of the whole number shall be necessary to a choice. But no person constitutionally ineligible to the office of President shall be eligible to that of Vice-President of the United States.[1]

The Electors shall meet in their respective states and vote by ballot for President and Vice-President, one of whom, at least, shall not be an inhabitant of the same state with themselves; they shall name in their ballots the person voted for as President, and in distinct ballots the person voted for as Vice-President, and they shall make distinct lists of all persons voted for as President, and of all persons voted for as Vice-President, and of the number of votes for each, which lists they shall sign and certify, and transmit sealed to the seat of the government of the United States, directed to the President of the Senate; -- the President of the Senate shall, in the presence of the Senate and House of Representatives, open all the certificates and the votes shall then be counted; -- The person having the greatest number of votes for President, shall be the President, if such number be a majority of the whole number of Electors appointed; and if no person have such majority, then from the persons having the highest numbers not exceeding three on the list of those voted for as President, the House of Representatives shall choose immediately, by ballot, the President. But in choosing the President, the votes shall be taken by states, the representation from each state having one vote; a quorum for this purpose shall consist of a member or members from two-thirds of the states, and a majority of all the states shall be necessary to a choice.

[And if the House of Representatives shall not choose a President whenever the right of choice shall devolve upon them, before the fourth day of March next following, then the Vice-President shall act as President, as in case of the death or other constitutional disability of the President.

--* The person having the greatest number of votes as Vice-President, shall be the Vice-President, if such number be a majority of the whole number of Electors appointed, and if no person have a majority, then from the two highest numbers on the list, the Senate shall choose the Vice-President; a quorum for the purpose shall consist of two-thirds of the whole number of Senators, and a majority of the whole number shall be necessary to a choice. But no person constitutionally ineligible to the office of President shall be eligible to that of Vice-President of the United States.

*Later Superseded by section 3 of the 20th amendment as follows:

20th Amendment

Section 3.
If, at the time fixed for the beginning of the term of the President, the President elect shall have died, the Vice President elect shall become President. If a President shall not have been chosen before the time fixed for the beginning of his term, or if the President elect shall have failed to qualify, then the Vice President elect shall act as President until a President shall have qualified; and the Congress may by law provide for the case wherein neither a President elect nor a Vice President shall have qualified, declaring who shall then act as President, or the manner in which one who is to act shall be selected, and such person shall act accordingly until a President or Vice President shall have qualified.

Explanation of 20th amendment

Before there were no airplanes, fast cars and fast railroads time was needed for new members and the new president to settle their affairs at home before traveling to Washington to join Congress,

March 4 was initially chosen as the date both a new president and Congress would take office. However, as transportation and communications improved, this meant that the departing Congress and president would remain in office for an unnecessarily long time following the November elections.

By moving the beginning of the president's new term from March 4 to January 20 (and in the case of Congress, to January 3), proponents of Amendment XX hoped to put an end to the "lame duck syndrome (where those who were not reelected had little power to push through their policies), while at the same time allowing for a speedier transition for the new administration and legislators. The amendment was ratified on January 23, 1933.

Amendment XX also provides for succession plans if the newly elected president or vice president is unable to assume his or her position. If the president is not able to hold office, the vice president will act as president.

Amendment XX also gives Congress the power to pass legislation outlining a more detailed succession plan if the vice president is also not able to carry out the presidential duties until a new president and vice president are qualified.

Chapter 7 The USA is a Constitutional Republic!

A representative democracy

We introduced the notion of a Republic as defined by the Constitution in Chapter 3. In this chapter, we expound on this notion.

The Constitution prescribes that the US is a representative democracy, which as you will see, along with having an elected chief executive, a voice for the minority, and a Constitution also makes the US a Republic. The pledge of allegiance notes the words: "…and to the Republic for which it stands," for our country is both a constitutional representative democracy and a Republic.

When we think of the very important notion that "America is a representative democracy," watching the "not-so-committed representatives" from both Parties who occupy our central government, it is a sane question to ask if this is really true.

The song, "Is that all there is?" comes to mind. Our generations are nothing like our parents and nothing like our Founders. We have reason to be ashamed of our government today, but we can be proud of our nation as of November 2016 as we did our best to get our country back on the right track.

Before this major glimmer of hope, our country was so far off the Founders' mark that even appropriate shame was no longer politically correct.

The faux battle of the Electoral College as the vehicle, which denied Hillary Clinton the presidency has been well refuted already in this book. As a master gamesperson, Mrs. Clinton knew when she went for the high stakes, such as the presidency, there would be rules in the contest to determine the winner. Even if the Pope and Jesus Christ suggested that the Electoral College was a bad idea to which anybody should agree, the fact is that both candidates agreed.

I know in my heart of hearts that Pope Francis, and Christ, my Savior would not eliminate a method needed to prevent a conspirator or a cheat to win the presidency, So I feel good about that. I feel good about the Electoral College.

If you are on the other side, then I am sure that you would like both of my witnesses to offer testimony. I regret that I can ask both but the only response would be able to come from the Pope, who is the Vicar of Christ on Earth.

This may do few people well as the term vicar itself may not be fully understood without explanation. So, here is a quick explanation:

In the Roman Catholic Church, a vicar is a representative or deputy of a bishop. The Pope is thus a representative or deputy of Jesus Christ, the Lord.

In the Episcopal Church, a vicar is a member of the clergy in charge of a chapel.

In the Church of England, a vicar is an incumbent of a parish where tithes formerly passed to a chapter or religious house or layman.

So, for Catholics, having both Christ and the Pope offer testimony would be redundant.

There is lots of confusion about whether the US is a democracy or a Republic. Let me solve the problem right here and now. It is both.

A representative democracy is the foundation of America. However, what makes America—America—is that we are also a Republic, the finest form of government ever brought forth from mankind.

We also have a set of laws, beginning with our Constitution, the primary law of the land. These laws govern all people and all politicians in perpetuity—as long as we hold politicians (aka representatives) accountable.

The simple definition of a Republic (from Latin -- res publica, meaning is as follows: *a state in which supreme power is held by the people and their elected representatives, and which has an elected or nominated president rather than a monarch.*

In practice in a Republic, the government is ruled by elected leaders who officiate according to law. The basic law in our country is the Constitution. Unlike a democracy, a Republic is not based on majority rule. The law of the land, a Constitution gives the minority a voice. Even a majority cannot supersede a constitutional principal, such as The Electoral College.

Our biggest and most important laws within the US Constitution are written so that the government cannot hurt the people (US) or impose its will upon US. It is not a trivial statement to say that "the people rule."

Our country was founded by some very smart people and they knew that without constraints on any government, which could potentially go wild and bad, the people would not be able to win. Even if the people are in the minority, if the majority is on the other side of the Constitution, the minority wins. That's why we have the Courts System to protect the rights of aggrieved minorities.

The constraints in the Constitution are implicit in that all the rights are owned by the people, and only those rights explicitly given to government are for the government.

Some presidents give lip service to the Constitution and do their own thing. That is why Donald J. Trump was the winner in 2016, in 30 of the 50 states. The people were sick of the lip service and the deceit of both parties.

In our time from 2014 to 2016, and for most of the Obama years. The people's rights have not counted for much. Obama's rights as an apparent dictator have been what has mattered. Republicans owned both houses of Congress but chose to let the Democrats run things. Specific Republicans careers ended because of this.

Republicans always seemed to back down fearing President Obama as an instrument of the people. Thinking Americans got fed up with Republicans cowering to Democrats on all issues and pledged to themselves that if a savior candidate for President ever came along, they would go for that candidate 100%.

Unfortunately, the Republican establishment elites proved they still have great disdain for the common people, such as you and I, the blokes who in 2010 had elected them to clean up the swamp. Many in their exclusive club, such as Mitt Romney, John McCain, Lyndsay Graham, Billy Crystol, Charles Krauthammer, and the biggest brain in the universe, George Will, turned on the people.

Other elites called Never Trumpers held major scorn for John Q. Public. They told we the people that our candidate was not worthy of our vote or anybody's vote. But, the people did not listen to the establishment Republican elites who nonetheless persisted in their vile, self-serving spew! Now as the swamp gets drained, they will be losing their power.

Long before the election of 2016, the full body of people in the US had gotten fed up with Barack Hussein Obama and Hillary Clinton and all of the dishonest liberal progressive communist politicians in America and their Republican sympathizers.

Though the press and the esteemed Republican establishment continued to tell we the people that Donald Trump was not worth our vote, the people used their brains and rejected the elite establishment and the Democrats such as Hillary Clinton.

We rejected the establishment on both sides and Donald Trump was the only good guy in town. God bless him in his victory! It makes a new breed of American very happy. We like the idea of America and Americans first! What's wrong with that?

Every now and then the other side wants to get on the right side. Who in good mind wants to be on the opposite side of American patriotic principles? All of these principles are embodied in the document—the great body of original law known as the United States Constitution. The Electoral College is a major part of this great document.

The love Americans have for the Constitution and its principles makes politicians and others—those more interested in government than the people the government serves—fear a backlash.

Why a backlash? When the corrupt office holders attempt to deny the people, even just one person, our liberty and freedom, that is cause for a revolution. Check out Thomas Jefferson's words in the Declaration of Independence. All Americans must pay attention to a potentially corrupt government.

In a pure democracy, if the majority decided that you or I should be killed, nothing would necessarily stop it. But, in a Republic, our form of government, it is the rule of law which prevails and the rule of law starts with the Constitution. The Majority is forbidden to vote to kill the minority.

The current president unfortunately has mocked the rule of law by operating lawlessly. Those days will end as President-elect Trump has promised. Barack Obama saw himself as a pert emperor and part dictator, so powerful that he operated in an extra-Constitutional fashion for many years.

Trump has pledged to end this tyranny and he intends to bring government back to the people. He won the election according to rules that were agreed upon by himself and Hillary Clinton.

Democrats, trying to subvert the constitutional principles that define how a President is to be elected, is a symptom of a far greater problem. Republicans, when they decide to use their guts, at least play by the law.

Obama has given Democrats an OK to operate outside the law. Do names such as Van Jones, Eric Holder, and my favorite candidate for US Tarmac Queen, Loretta Lynch, mean anything to ordinary people? I must say "yes" because the people, by voting for Donald Trump, have given the boot to those supporting officials such as these few, who are OK with tyrannical and subversive activity.

Until Obama, I had never witnessed an Attorney General being so biased in favor of the Administration that it affected their judgment.

It seems for sure that many in our nation today, mostly on the far left, have been trying real hard to kill America's America by demeaning the Constitution and the Bill of Rights in particular. You more than likely selected this book to help fight them off before it happens. Thank you.

If you could figure any way to put an unmovable grip on corrupt politicians, right now or in the future, would you not do it? The Founders of America put a stranglehold on all corrupt political agents of the future when they wrote and adopted the US Constitution, the greatest body of law ever written in any civilization. Bad people should be able to be prosecuted under US Law but this can only happen if the Attorney General is not corrupt.

Of course, if we the people do not know what is written in the Constitution, it cannot help us much. Can it? The Electoral College is just one item of importance. There are many.

So, it is time for all Americans who have not been paying attention to stop being dummmies, and pure political sport for the elite. It is time to rule America as our birthright as citizens of this great country commands US. Let somebody else eat cake!

And, so, my fellow Americans, that is the number one reason that in order to form a more perfect union of the original thirteen colonies / states, and with more states expected after the first thirteen, our forefathers built the finest Constitution ever fashioned by the pen of human hands.

I love to repeat that The Bible, from the hand of God, may be the greatest story ever told in the greatest book ever written, but the Constitution is as good as it gets for the goodness of man, written by the hands of our first patriots. Surely this document was written with the guidance of God.

In this day and age, there are everyday attempts by the government, for years under the control of the Democratic Party, to undermine our lasting Republic. We now all know that our country is an almost pure constitutional representative democracy—with the minority having a voice right along with the majority. The attacks on this Republic most often come from the left and alt left side of the political spectrum.

Democrats can be better patriots for sure. They should be. Why do they choose to be anti-American? I do know? Their leaders do not tell them the truth.

Katie Kieffer TownHall.com strikes a chord

On September 19, almost two months before the 2016 election, Katie Kieffer of townhall.com struck a great chord with her expose on Hillary Clinton's attack on what HRC calls the alt-right.

Alt-right has been twisted by Democrats and HRC today to mean a soft bigotry. whereas "alt-left" quite accurately describes the political ideology of today's Democratic Party.

Hillary Clinton recently told a crowd of college students in Reno, NV: "Race-baiting ideas. Anti-Muslim and anti-immigrant ideas—[are] all key tenets making up an emerging racist ideology known as the 'alt-right."

Hillary Clinton of course stole the term "alt-right"from the inimitable Patrick J. Buchanan and has bastardized its historical meaning. The term had been created as an alternative to mainstream conservatism in much the way as Buchanan's libertarian-conservatism.

Rather than create their own term, today's Democrats have decided to coopt the term "alt-right" pejoratively. They more than imply that if you support Donald Trump, you're a white supremacist. Case closed. I suppose if you are alt-left, then you are anti-white, and pro-everything else.

Kieffer suggests that a strong offense is the best defense when fighting bullies. Her offensive move is to turn Hillary's words against her. She calls them the alternative-left "alt-left." They are the fallen angels from the one-time pragmatic Democratic ideals of John F. Kennedy and they have now embraced a radical "power at any cost" fringe philosophy of Saul Alinsky and Bill Ayers. It works for me because it is true and very insightful.

The whole notion of the disrespect for the Constitution's Electoral College, and the validity of the votes in just states that Trump won, and not in those where Hillary had a slight margin is a manifestation of the alt-left in full regalia. For example Hillary won New Hampshire by 2700 votes and the Republicans did not ask for a recount.

Alt left behavior is often associated with lying. Lying about intentions is still lying. President Obama made his final comment on recounts and the Electoral College on November 14 at a press conference: "Look, the people have spoken. Donald Trump will be the next President, the 45th President of the United States." In her concession speech, Clinton said, "Donald Trump is going to be our president" and added that Americans "respect and cherish" the "rule of law." So, why the change? Was she kidding? No, she was serious but this is typical alt-left behavior.

So it is not surprising to anybody just learning about the alt-left, that the alt-left are not America's finest. Katie Kieffer offered a number of examples in her piece about alt-left extremist behavior. Her conclusion is that "the radical measures that today's Democratic Party supports demonstrate that they have morphed into a fringe group."

With whites of both sexes being the majority in the country, the fringe might be defined as all-others. For example, when have you last seen a Democrat trying to appeal to white voters? Hillary mentions white supremacists in her definition of the alt-right. Though not correct, it would be more correct if she just said "white."

Here are some other things Kieffer notes that the alt-left loves to support:

1.) **Ignore Science**: Hillary Clinton opposed the construction of the Keystone Pipeline even though her own State Dept. three times declared it to be environmentally safe.

2.) **Pretend States Don't Exist**: Obama's administration sued Arizona for exercising its own immigration laws; North Carolina over its bathroom laws.

3.) **Coddling Thugs, Killing Free Speech:** SyedRizwan Farook and Tashfeen Malik stormed a gun free zone in San Bernardino, CA last December—fatally shooting 14 individuals and injuring 24. U.S. Attorney General Loretta Lynch threatened to prosecute anyone who dared say anything that could be in any way construed as anti-Muslim—despite Farook and Malik being radicalized jihadist Muslims.

4.) **Crushing Bakeries and Pizzerias:** Alt-left protesters put a bakery out of business when the owner practiced her 1st Amendment right to free speech.

5.) **No ID to Vote:** Democrats do not want to know who is voting. Could politicians want to hide their attempts to buy votes from illegal immigrants?

6.) **Double Standards:** A Marine gets court-martialed for taking six pictures for his mom in a submarine but HRC has no charges filed for far more serious security violations

Etc. There are many others You can see Katie Kieffer's piece at townhall.com. September 19, 2016

There is a lot of hypocrisy in the Democratic party that is now run by the alt-left. While their leaders become billionaires, the normal people in the Democratic neighborhoods suffer low wages and have a tough time making ends meet. Democrat leaders are hypocrites to their own supporters. That's why I left the Party in spirit though I am still a Democrat by registration.

Because Obama has shut down the economy, he must give the people alms from the US treasury to keep their loyalty. Theoretically, this is to help them overcome their adversity.

The truth is that all people should be angry with this one-time president, knowing that he is *the-who* that intentionally caused their adversity in the first place. Obama could have done much better. His ideology and scorn for American traditions pushed him towards me-first ideology-driven actions.

Democracy is the opposite of communism

The ideology of the progressive left (alt-left) favors Marxism and its simpler forms of socialism and communism. Since Americans do not typically vote for socialists, communists, or Marxists, other than some who voted for Bernie Sanders rather than Hillary Clinton, these are notions that nobody other than a crooked politician would want.

No politician wanting to be elected will admit they are more communist than American. Yet, as much as it pains me to tell you, unfortunately, they are!

These overtures, which demean the Constitution, the fabric of our democracy, originate from corrupt politicians who have been caught up in an alt leftist movement, which would like to end capitalism, and bring on a socialist / communist order to replace the American Dream, and all the dreams of *We the People*! The attack on the Electoral College is just one of many.

Our Republic as noted, is a representative democracy constrained by laws and a separation of powers. The Constitution is the biggest constraint that prohibits government from taking over your life—and that is good. Yet, we do have representatives. But, they too-often choose to treat us as dummmies.

Those of us who supported Donald Trump as a change agent for America feel we now have a chance to make America great again. We'll be watching Mr. Trump very closely

If we believe, it can be made a reality. And, we should scream it out at the polling places and at our representative's offices as often as we can. We should accept nothing less. Americans rule America. It is our birthright given to us by the Founders, and chronicled in the US Constitution.

The people have the responsibility for keeping government honest!

It is up to all people in this great country to understand our laws, first the Constitution. Then, we must pay attention that our leaders follow those laws.

When the top officials in our government do not follow the laws of the land, we must learn to send them home every two, four, or six years, as determined by their term lengths as set forth in the Constitution for our House (2 years), the President (4 years), and the Senate (6 years) respectively. Scoundrels should get no repeat performances.

So, don't give up! Do not let the politicians think they run the country! The Founders hated both big-time and petty politicians whose missions were to thwart the will of the people.

That is why our government has worked well for over 225 years. When we get bad apples, we throw them away by voting them out. Of course, that means we must vote in order for our choices to matter. And we must be willing to vote our own representatives from our home locations, in the House or the Senate out of office when they choose to not do their jobs. Americans showed we care in the 2016 election and that is a good thing.

Representatives are of the people-- maybe?

Though the representatives are supposed to come from the people, a type of political class of elites has come about and seldom do we get to vote for representatives, anymore, who are willing to represent the people's interests. We get career politicians instead.

By understanding America better, and especially by understanding our Constitution, Americans have a far better chance of bringing good and honest government back to the people.

We must not be afraid of casting out the evil politicians in our government, even if they have given our families favors. Favors are the devil's trick of dirty politicians. They think they can get us all one at a time. Let's send all these bad guys packing.

The Constitution provides that elected officials are given the task to coordinate our pooled resources for the intended benefit of "everyone." But everyone is often not included. And politicians often take credit for spending scarce treasury dollars on things that simply buy themselves votes.

Nobody wants this and so it is up to all of us to change it. The Trump revolution is a magnificent first step but the wake-up call of the people will need much more time. Donald Trump needs our full support for him to succeed for us.

Do representatives care?

Do our representatives have a genuinely compelling concern for the people and our government or is this simply our impossible dream of Nirvana?

Our government leaders have chosen at multiple, levels to be wholly unaccountable to We the People. Today, our government leaders reject the fundamental principles of our founding and their government has no real legitimacy the further it drifts from the precepts of the Constitution.

The US was not designed this way. The Constitution is the blueprint for our Country's design. It was designed by a group of artisans to not only represent their artistic touch, but to be held as the behavioral creed of the people, for the people, and by the people, forever. What thinking human being blessed to be part of America, could ask for anything more?

If you think that life, freedom, liberty, and the ability to pursue your own happiness are simple notions, and givens in any civilization, get out your thinking cap, and think again.

Why do people from all over the world crash our gates just to get in? Americans are exceptional in that we have full freedom and liberty in our country, and with that we can exceed all limits. Go to any other country, and this exception no longer applies.

Traditionally, the USA has been the freest nation in the world with rights withheld from government and rights given to the people by our Constitution. Today as our country's foundation is being threatened from within, more than likely you are reading about the Electoral College, just a small piece of our noble Constitution so you can help protect your rights as well as this great nation which provides them.

Which would you first give up? Your freedom? Your life? Your liberty? Your family? Or your ability to do what you need to do to be happy? The sanest answer of course is "none of the above."

Who could ask for anything better than being an American? Ask the last arriving immigrant! We are free! But, if Americans do not care about our founding precepts, maybe our freedom, our lives, our liberty, our families, our sacred honor, and our ability to do what we need to do to be happy, will be taken from us one day—perhaps in the not-too-distant future.

If the design of our nation, America, which the Founders labored to create is so great, you might ask, why is it that our current lawmakers ignore it? Republicans and Democrats alike appear to be indifferent to the needs of the people they represent. Why?

The true answer to that question is very unfortunate for Americans. There is tacit collaboration in undermining the principles of our Democratic Republic by our supposed representatives, their supporters, the special interests, corporate interests and worse of all, the fourth estate aka the today's corrupt press. All of these factions were against Donald Trump in 2016, and we the people won a grand victory. Let's keep at it!

We the people are sick of coming in last. Before Trump's election, politicians believed that we were not paying attention. Maybe we had not been paying enough attention. This is about to end. Paying attention is about to become the motto of the free and the brave! Welcome and thank you, Mr. Trump.

Chapter 8 Legitimate Immigration Was Necessary

Is immigration still necessary?

Americans are all pro-immigration to the extent of our laws and our needs as a country. If Americans were not pro-immigration for example, Columbus and his shipmates and their families more than likely would have withered away from disease or cold winters or they would have lost their battles with Native Americans.

All fifty states; at least the mainland forty-eight, would probably now have Native American names, and they would be run by the same financial wizards who run today's highly successful casinos.

After the USA was in operation as a country with a Constitution for just several years, its population was approaching 4 million people. This is just a million more people than the annual flow of illegal immigrants from south of the border.

On March 26, 1790, just more than 225 years ago, the second session of the first Congress (operating under the Constitution with a House and a Senate) approved the new nation's initial effort to create the rules under which foreign-born persons could become U.S. citizens.

From this point on, our borders were not open per se, and we had laws (rules) for how those wishing to be Americans could come to visit or to become Americans. All Americans after this point, who immigrated, were to follow the laws of the land. The Constitution was the supreme law of the land followed by federal laws, the state laws and then local laws. Today, our most recent past president along with Congress have decided not to enforce many of the laws that are on the books.

The Naturalization Act of 1790 specified that "any alien, being a free white person," could apply for citizenship, so long as he or she lived in the United States for at least two years, and in the state where the application was filed for at least a year. It took the US a while to do the right thing for former slaves. But, eventually, over 150 years ago, we got it right.

The new law also provided that "children of citizens of the United States that may be born ... out of the limits of the United States shall be considered as natural born citizens." Over the next thirty to seventy years, the Congress cleaned up the immigration laws so that all original residents of America, whether African or Native American were Americans – including former slaves.

In effect, the law originally left out indentured servants, slaves, and most women. But, it was improved. Just like Windows 10.0 was introduced over 30 years after Windows 1. Our immigration laws improved via from version 1 to the current version via thoughtful iterations.

These laws also mandated that one must "absolutely and entirely renounce and abjure all allegiance and fidelity to every foreign Prince, Potentate, State or Sovereignty." Though these terms were seen as quite generous, still the law denied the right to naturalize to "persons whose fathers have never been resident in the United States."

Immigration law was becoming more important and the laws have been changed several times since 1790. For example, in 1795, as anti-immigrant feeling began to grow, the necessary period of residence to become a citizen was increased from two to five years. Sometimes the US has needed immigrants and sometimes not. In all cases, it should not be the immigrant's decision, it is the decision of the citizens of the United States. Immigration law became more firm as the nation aged and the leaders concern was focused on Americans and American interests.

Enter special interests, who like to bypass laws and have their friendly "owned" politicians let them get away with whatever. Regarding immigration, you already know that there are two major special interests. The first special interest is the Democratic Party, which operates as if all illegal foreign nationals should immediately be made citizens.

Smart Democrat politicos favor this because they feel the Democrat Party would never lose another election. That is a great motivator to bring all foreigners in immediately and make them all citizens of this nation.

Democrats no longer care about the families of citizens that built America and the families of citizens that have lived for a hundred or more years in America. That is why many Democrats said good-by to the Party of the fringe in this past election.

And, so, even though they have taken American jobs and driven down the average weekly wage, your Democratic Representatives in Congress still advocate amnesty and citizenship for them, promising less prosperity for all American citizens. When Americans ae unemployed we do not need immigration—legal or illegal.

Unfortunately, most Americans, not seeing that their representatives have become corrupt with socialist and communist leanings, looking for a poor continually underserved underclass, will vote them back into office to their own peril. It is time rank and file Democrats realize their Democratic

Leadership has abandoned them—especially, I say with much chagrin, if you are a non-Hispanic Caucasian.

The major concern of corrupt politicians is that the Democrat members of Congress get reelected. We can put a period there. But, they also work hard so that a Democrat president can be elected each time. Bringing in poor people from south of the border, who feed from our welfare system, assures the Democratic politicians of their votes.

The second special interest is also against the people. They do not gain at the ballot box. However, illegal foreign nationals do provide huge gains for the wallets of American businessmen, who care nothing about regular Americans—the John Does like you and I out there.

American businesses, represented today by the elite Republican establishment, love paying the smallest wage possible and providing the smallest amount of benefits possible. Since illegal foreign nationals work for peanuts, this is a perfect marriage of needs.

Traditional Republicans have great alliances with businesses. The only groups, who align with the majority of Americans, and who oppose blanket amnesty, and who are 100% pro-American citizen—philosophically—are the conservatives, nationalists, and populists. They were once identified by their claim of allegiance to the now defunct TEA Party. Now, we are all pleased to be Trumpists. Donald Trump is one of the most remarkable men ever in America. His popularity in December of 2016, over a month before his inauguration is through the roof.

The conservatives, nationalists, and populists, differ on immigration with elitist Republicans, and opportunist Democrats. No American citizen suffering from the worst economy since the depression would be asking the government to invite more wage lowering workers into America.

After Republicans chose to side with Democrats once the Lincoln Party became the majority in the House and Senate, it was a big blow for those of us who are for America First. Tea Party advocates have simply gone underground in disgust. Many of the same people who once made up the Tea Party transformed from idealistic Tri-cornered hat wearing patriots, who believed that Republican campaign rhetoric mirrored their beliefs, into nationalists and populists. Like yours truly.

They are anti-establishment and anti-elite and in many ways we simply want a better America. We really do not care if Republicans or Democrats win as long as the people win.

This leftover group that is no longer a group, but a bunch of individual thinkers, have become a much savvier and in some ways a much more cynical electorate. That is why Donald Trump has become our President-elect. The elitist establishment Republicans are held in poor regard by most informed citizens.

The Chamber hates John Q. Public.

Thomas J. Donahue, President of the US Chamber of Congress, a disgusting voice for the establishment, told Republican lawmakers that if they did not pass amnesty, the Republicans shouldn't even bother to run a candidate in 2016.

Populist and Nationalist conservatives got the message loud and clear that establishment Republicans could not be trusted. They have been trying to undercut Donald Trump from the first moment that it appeared that he was the favorite son of the people.

Please note that when I say populist and nationalist, I am not suggesting that does not include the notion of Republicanism. I am not suggesting that I am for populist majoritarian rule. As I have noted several times in this book, I believe in our Republic and our principles as a constitutional representative democracy that provides a minority voice.

The Chamber of Commerce as far as I am concerned is a subversive group in the same vein as the Democratic Party. They care nothing about America and everyday Americans.

They care nothing about workers' salaries but care a lot about corporate profits. Donohue demanded that lawmakers pass amnesty or they would receive no funding from the Chamber for their reelections. Observing the establishment has begun to make populist nationalists and conservatives suffer from nausea in disgust.

Most Americans are aware that our Senate lifted the ruse of being for the people about three years ago. The US Senate, then controlled by Democrats and RINOS , passed a global amnesty bill in 2013, and they were pressuring the House of Representatives to do the same.

The essence of the bill was that illegal foreign nationals would be coddled and loved by our government (the theoretical majority). Illegal foreign nationals would be given a higher stature in life than American Citizens trying to eke out a family wage.

Thank You, Lord, for big things—the conservatives in the House would not budge thankfully. Of course, if they were ever to have passed this scourge on America, just as Marco Rubio got whooped by Trump and others in the 2016 Primaries, the people would have revolted sooner.

With no excuses left, steady voters and formerly non-voters would have thrown out both houses of Congress and started over. The people have lots of power when we "pay attention." Donald Trump's election is a result of a majority of American citizens paying more attention. We really want the SWAMP to be drained. That means many politicos still need to be sent home, and never brought back to D.C.

The immigration issue is being put forth in this book as another of the issues such as the Electoral College. It is just another issue that the bad guys want to go their way so they can control all Americans and keep us in poverty. Then, when they pass out the bones and table scraps, we will appreciate them and say thank you to the Democrat leaders and cast our votes for them again. Not me! Never again! Hopefully not you!

There are lots of examples in which Democrats and RINOS have tried to undermine the rule of law. The Gang of Eight Bill and the behavior of the elitists in both Parties shows that before Trump (BT), our legislators cared more about other factors such as reelection and donations than they did about the people. I expect that to change with the reintroduction of shame.

We need no more immigration—legal or illegal for a while for sure. We have enough people in the country right now or else our real unemployment picture would not look so bad. Why bring more "slave labor" into the country when we know it will make the problem of making ends meet for American families that much more difficult?

Like many, I hear the Wall Street Journal Republican Elitists crying that by getting jobs for 1100 Carrier employees will kill the incentive for businesses to operate in America. They are so self-serving it stinks. The Wall Street Journal and the Chamber of Commerce represent the Swamp folks. It helps to know that.

If US businesses believe they cannot survive when the citizens of the US have nice high paying jobs, then I would be the first to help these businesses get out of business or at least get out of our country sooner than later. This is not a country about business for business and too bad if corporations are hurt when their sting on US employees is ended. If your company cannot compete in America with American labor and yet you expect Americans to buy your products, go out of business, please!

Many Americans do not care if Samsung or Nokia or Whoverokia chooses to employ citizens of the US in the USA, at a respectable wage. The people want companies to oprate in the US whther owned by Americans or foreign nationals. We are for job providers rather than the anti-American supposed American companies.

I would love to see companies such as those above making clone Apples or IBMs in America protected from the laws that today keep them from doing so. I would love to see Donald Trump's administration choosing not to take issue with US copyrights, trademarks, and patents for foreign companies willing to build plants in the US and employ US workers—if the holder of the patent has taken operations offshore.

Why would a President Trump take issue with companies who make competitive products to IBM or Apple in the US if unlike Apple and IBM, they hire American labor in America?

Any company such as IBM or Apple that cannot be good to American workers should be declared a foreign country. Any foreign country that makes a substantial portion of its product in the good ole USA should be declared an American company.

American companies (those operating in America) will pay the new lower corporate tax rate. Non-American companies, such as IBM and Apple and lots others should pay the foreign tax rate as well as a nice tariff to bring products into the U.S. In this way, we can thank foreign companies for building plants, hiring Americans, and operating in the USA.

Call it a tariff if you will but the fact is that tariffs under the 18th century mercantilism rules were always put forth to protect US companies from foreign companies. The irony today is that American employees want to be protected from American companies that do not consider their impact on American employees.

Such companies want the people's representatives to give them the rights to take advantage of the very people (you, me, and your brother) that the government of the US should be helping.

This book is not about immigration or the economy per se, but they are related as both are governed by the Constitution. The Electoral College issue is about some people wanting to take Donald Trump's victory away. That is not going to happen. If it happened, all the good we are discussing above cannot happen.

We need Donald Trump more than ever. We need him to fulfill his promises. Most Americans are not worried about the Electoral College and the attacks of Democrats on our Constitution. If somehow, through their shenanigans the Democrats found a judge somewhere with the power to make Hillary our President. I predict there would be a country full of protesters on the street—not just those being paid $750 per week by the Democrats and their donor base.

We would be looking for Jefferson's advice in the Declaration of Independence to get us back on track.

Chapter 9   Why Does The Constitution Matter?

Electoral College is Just one more victim

There is a quiet undertone in the Democratic Party that suggests that the Consitution no longer matters. President Barack Obama in his time, created one lawless anti-Constitutional Executive Order after another with impunity The Democrats seem to have taken to the new lawlessness as a badge of honor that their ideas are somehow better than the Constitution. Their attempts to minimize the Founders' Electoral College because it would be convenient for Mrs. Clinton are a continuation of their contempt for the Greatest Law of the Land.

Republicans have been too agreeable to the new Democrats who want everything their way. Before Mr. Trump, the Establishment Elite Republicans stood back and chose not to be the opposition Party. Even after they got the power in 2012, they let the Democrats get away with every trick in the book and would not lift a finger to stop them to—even to help the Country recover. There was no fight in the wimpy RINOS that ran the Party. Their donor base was everything and the people meant nothing to them.

Part of the natural prescription the Founders gave citizens of this great country to assure good government was frequent elections. Yet, somehow, our representatives have figured out how simply by doing their jobs in special constituent matters, they could gain favor and be reelected even if they did a poor job for the rest of America. This is the fault of a far too complacent, non-vigilant constituency – you and I and the guy next door.

The Democrats and Greens and others pushing the idea of the popular vote, and suing the state and federal government for recounts of an already decided election is met well by the Trump organization. However, not enough Republicans have been standing up to stop this ludicracy.

Our representatives are in office far too long and they gain relationships with other politicians. They make up a new class known as the ruling class, who are funded by the bag men—a.k.a.—the donor class.

Instead of thinking about the folks in South Bend, or Scranton, or Clarks-Summit, or Santa Rosa, or New York, or Plymouth, Reno, Yellowstone, or Kinston, our esteemed national politicians too-soon begin to think they belong in Washington DC, not their home cities. They become "special" people. They see themselves as a cut above mere mortal men.

The social life in DC is lots better than most home towns, and our devoted representatives get to rub elbows with the hoity-toity, and the progressive Marxist communists that do not exist in their home areas. They get corrupted quickly and they seem to enjoy it. Shame on them.

All of a sudden they are important. Being from Podunk or Pittsburgh does not matter. They begin to like the trappings of Washington more than being with their loved ones back in their home states. They forget their mission is to represent US and not themselves.

They try very hard to please the lobbyists and the communists and even those on the other team. They want to be liked and they want something in return that they don't get from the home town folks. Sometimes it is gifts; sometimes it is invitations to the best Parties, and sometimes it is the promise of a great job as a lobbyist if not reelected. The longer they are in Congress or in politics per se, the greater the opportunity for corruption. It is tough to resist and therefore, many succumb to the temptations, and become god-like when they return to their home town.

Unfortunately for all Americans, the new "important" relationships override the notion of fair representation for the people (US) from back home. When they take their oaths of office and they promise to represent US, most are sincere at the time. That may be the last time. Just because the Electoral College is part and parcel of the Constitution, and they have sworn to uphold the Constitution does not mean their other interests would not override their responsibilities.

Once they come to Washington, they experience the trappings and the temptations. And, because humans are only human, way too many of our finest stray from the mark and contribute to the re-creation of a country of which few thinking Americans are proud today.

It is too bad that we Americans are either too kind or not enough self-assured that we keep "trusting" these scoundrels even after innumerable lies and self-aggrandizement. We can't believe they would do "that." Yet they do. So, like dummmies, we go ahead and we call them hizzoner or herronner and we reelect them because we think they really cannot be that bad. And, then again there is that favor they did five years ago! Will a new guy be so kind?

Ladies and gentlemen, they are that bad. Stop electing them. Thankfully we stopped the presidential pattern in which the political Parties, who do not have our interests at heart, once picked the presidents and made us think it was US. Donald Trump really upsets them all. They would love to get him on a technicality, such as a fraudulent recount or an executive order to ignore the Electoral College.

Though he is a billionaire and can be as hoity-toity as he chooses, Mr. Trump has decided to be of the hoi polloi. He is so affable that if Trump liked beer, I would send him an invitation to one of our family celebrations and he would enjoy himself like one of the family. I may invite him anyway.

The biggest fear of the elite establishment politician is that someday all Americans will understand the Constitution chapter and verse. On that day, we will have all the rights, and they will have zero.

Think about our forefathers, especially George Washington, who guided our troops in the revolution against England's tyranny. Think about honest Abe Lincoln, who freed the slaves and saved the union. They would weep to see what their political successors, our representatives, have done to our nation.

So, our fair-haired representatives choose to represent themselves and their special interests, rather than the areas of the country that sent them to the Congress of the USA to represent the people. Perhaps a dose of Lincoln's "honesty," is all that is needed to save the day. Wouldn't that be nice?

Our "honorables," do not even seem to care for our well-being. They do, however, care for their leadership positions, which make them big shots. They care for themselves for sure. Unfortunately, they just can't get it into their heads that we the people are the reason they are in their positions in the first place.

We the people are the employers of all members of Congress, and they serve at our pleasure. In our Republic, our government does not rule over us; it serves us, according to the laws that we ask our representatives to make on our behalf. The President as the Executive is responsible for law enforcement. Every now and then we have to remind them of their jobs. When they choose not to listen, we must fire them.

The more we all understand that the tighter the reins we can place on errant politicians, the more the people are in charge. It is not too late. The Constitution is our guide and it is our license to rid ourselves of a poor government.

We must understand the Constitution for it to work again for US and for America. The last thing we should consider doing is to permit corrupt politicians, which we unfortunately have already elected to serve the people, to disembody our Constitution through legislation or through executive actions.

A big part of the problem is our fault since we do not check them out well enough before we vote them into office. To make it simple to understand this notion—if there is a rotten piece of fish in the market and we select it for dinner, whose fault is it when it doesn't taste so good and our guests get sick? So, when we pick a rotten person to represent US—whose fault is that? You see, we do not have to be dummmies. Too often, however, we choose to be.

Does it matter whether the government is controlled by Democrats or Republicans? Democratic leaders have become socialist progressives, just this side of communists over the past several years. The Democrats at home are not far leftists but their leaders are. Republicans still seem to love the American way and are not moving the country towards communism. But, Republicans are too passive in dealing with Democratic leadership that appears hell-bent on destroying our country.

Our country's destruction rate grows at a higher rate when leftist progressive communists are in office. When Republicans take over, though it lessens, it does not go to zero as it should because too many elite establishment Republicans have quietly become progressives and they sympathize with the opposition. Again, we populist nationalists expect that Donald Trump will solve this one for us.

So, right now at least, Republicans, especially conservative Republicans are a better choice for America than Democrats. As a conservative Democrat, myself, that is very tough for me to say. I wish it were not so. I do remember when the Democrats were the Party of the people.

Today, the best thing for America is to vote for conservatives, and populist nationalists who also love and respect the Constitution--even if they are Democrat. But, the facts show most conservatives are either Republican or Libertarian.

The people have been short-changed on the notion of representation and honesty. Honesty is the first thing to go when a representative must lie in order to get the extra benefits their positions can deliver. We voted all of these 545 miscreants to run our government. We get the government we deserve.

My objective in writing is to do my best to remove low-information voters by creating high information patriots. If I can help smarten up a lot of people, such as your uncle Ben, so that guys like that, whether they are the president or not, do not get to treat you like a chump, I have done a lot for mankind.

Each time I write about any topic, I too get smarter. We all must keep learning all our lives and we must be watchful for dishonest politicians so that we can keep our freedoms.

America is built on fairness, goodness, and individual strength. We are not supposed to give politicians an even break. The Constitution is our law and it is our obligation to pay attention so our rights are not violated by grabby politicians.

If you happen to be in this low information / overly nice category, thank you for visiting this book. I hope that through these writings, you will become a better American.

The low information gullible people in America must smarten up or over time, we are all toast. Everybody's vote counts the same. When those who choose to not pay attention vote, it is a big plus for dirty politicians and a big loss for real Americans.

My tell-all book on the Constitution called *The Constitution 4 Dummmies*, is written so that we can all know the truth even when the corrupt media lies to our faces.

Today, the not-so-free, very dishonest, corrupt and biased press provides cover for liberal progressives as an ally, not as the fourth estate. It is propaganda for the government and too many gullible Americans sop it up as if it is the truth. The media would have us all believe in the "Tooth Fairy."

Any of US that live by believing their lies, need to reevaluate so that we do not remain chumps.

Illegal immigration and amnesty are two other bad jokes perpetrated on the American people by corrupt politicians. In this instance, both the Democrats and the Republicans share the same vision – *to stiff the American people,* and to give priority to illegal foreign nationals rather than American citizens. What happened to America and Americans first?

Some truths stand forever. Even today's president, when he met with Pope Francis could not think of anything positive to say, so he quoted his buddy Harry Reid as you can see in the "cartoon" below. The bubbled exchange with the Pope is funny but too true. Pope Francis must have a great sense of humor. Don't we just love his simplicity?

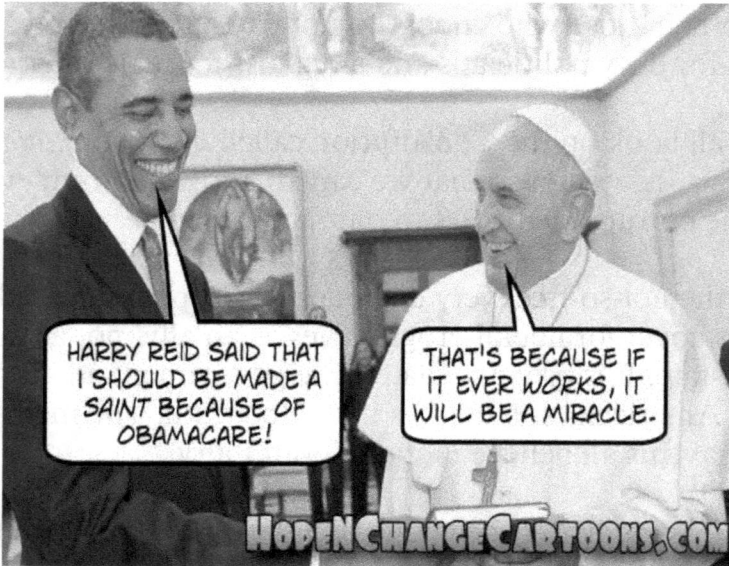

HARRY REID SAID THAT I SHOULD BE MADE A SAINT BECAUSE OF OBAMACARE!

THAT'S BECAUSE IF IT EVER WORKS, IT WILL BE A MIRACLE.

HopeNChangeCartoons.com

It should be easy for Americans to believe in the Constitution because it is our book of freedoms. We have all the power and the government has just what we choose to give it. Those with little respect for the Constitution would like to give government all power. They would have no problem getting rid of separation of powers, the Electoral College, citizenship, and anything else that is in the way of the progressive socialist alt-left agenda.

I am a registered Democrat but for thirty years or more, I have not been proud of my Party. The Democratic leadership can do a lot better. Right now, the Party that is the lesser of two evils is unquestionably the Republican Party though it is an unholy combination of both Democrats and Republicans that have given us this sad state of affairs in the USA.

Will Donald Trump cure it all? Maybe not but; I can feel the freshness and cleanness in the country already with this new huge broom coming into the Oval Office. A new broom sweeps clean.

Without using these exact words, our Constitution gives us a government of the people, by the people, and for the people. It gives government only powers that are specifically enumerated by the people. Yet, somehow, many Americans have become lazy and we have permitted corrupt politicians to be reelected regardless of whether they represent US well or not.

Abraham Lincoln is the most famous historical figure to use this patriotic phrase. It was in his Gettysburg Address from November 19, 1863. For posterity, here is Lincoln's last paragraph. It is chilling:

"It is rather for us to be here dedicated to the great task remaining before us -- that from these honored dead we take increased devotion to that cause for which they gave the last full measure of devotion -- that we here highly resolve that these dead shall not have died in vain -- that this nation, under God, shall have a new birth of freedom -- and that government of the people, by the people, for the people, shall not perish from the earth."

Big government doesn't work. Big agencies don't work. Big corporations don't work. Big doesn't work well at all, especially if you are one American citizen looking for freedom and liberty.

Government has grown so big that we the people, who own the government according to a deed known as the Constitution, can no longer sort through all the lies and the empty promises. So, we must all help reduce the size of government for the people to ever matter again. We get our chances each election cycle. When we vote to favor corruption, we get the government we deserve.

If all Americans understood America, and were taught to respect America in our schools, instead of blaming America first for everything—we would not have to worry about being defeated from within.

In this way, if any American political Party comes-by led by Democrats or Republicans, and it wants to change America into a Communist-Russian-like, or Communist-Chinese-like, or

Nazi-German-like country, we will be equipped to fire off a quick nyet, or a mhai, or simply, a hearty and guttural nein!

We cannot accept and believe the propaganda from the corrupt, socialist progressive communist owned alt-left press in the US. Yes, that includes the New York Times, the Washington Post and of course MSNBC. Trying to find the truth in today's news is like trying to find a white glove in the snow or a black glove in an oil sludge.

America, from its inception, along with mercantilism, has used capitalism to create the strongest country in the world. Those who do not like America have already removed mercantilism from the landscape and now hope to replace capitalism with socialism / communism. Yet, small-c-communism has never worked anyplace.

Chapter 10 Read the Federalist Papers

Intended to convince New Yorkers to vote for the Constitution

Before I wrote the very patriotic "4 Dummmies" series, my last book was titled *The Federalist Papers, by Hamilton, Jay, and Madison*. Shortly thereafter, I also wrote a book titled *The Federalist Papers Companion* to help readers more easily navigate the Federalist Papers. Both books are availaable at amazon.com/author/brianwkelly

Since these eloquent Founders—Alexander Hamilton, John Jay, and James Madison—had already written the papers, my job was merely to arrange them in a 21st century orderly style and set them to print. As an introduction, I put together about twenty pages of original material to help persuade the potential reader that the Federalist papers are the Real Deal. There are lots of learning opportunities about our government in the Federalist Papers

I took these 85 patriotic essays of Alexander Hamilton, John Jay, and James Madison, known as The Federalist Papers, and I separated all of the two page and single page paragraphs, and half page paragraphs, and other very large paragraphs, and made them more readable without changing a word.

I chopped the essays into smaller, more readable bits and pieces. My twenty-page exclusive introduction plus the reformatting differentiate my version from others. My version is

available in paperback or Kindle book from
amazon.com/author/brianwkelly.

If you can get by without the reformatting and the explanatory
introduction, you can get the Federalist Papers for free on the
Internet from many sources. There is a lot of learning to be had
in the Federalist Papers. Navigating the long paragraphs in the
original for some may be a chore. I would recommend typing in
Federalist Papers in your web browser before you spend a dime
and begin to read the essays. It may be all you need. Here is one
free source in case your search is not successful:

http://www.foundingfathers.info/federalistpapers/fedi.htm

The Federalist Papers are a series of 85 articles and essays,
written by Founders Alexander Hamilton, James Madison, and
John Jay. The essays originally appeared anonymously in
New York newspapers in 1787 and 1788 under the pen
name "**Publius**.", a sixth century Roman patriot, general, and
statesman.

The purpose of the Federalist authors was to convince the
people that the best course of action was to ratify the US
Constitution. There were also anti-federalist position essays
available during the same time period. These are also available
on the internet for free.

The Federalist Papers were original submissions to several New
York newspapers so they would be read by the masses and the
idea was that the masses would support the Consitution.
Reading the Federalist Papers today is a must for every US
citizen.

The Electoral College Federalist # 68 Summary

Federalist Number 68 is the sixty-eighth essay of The Federalist
Papers. It was more than likely written by Alexander Hamilton,

though like all the Federalist Papers it was signed, *Publius.* It was submitted on March 12, 1788.

Entitled "The Mode of Electing the President," this essay describes Hamilton's view of the process for selecting the Chief Executive of the United States of America.

Hamilton was a prolific writer and wrote most of the Federalist Papers. His objective as noted previously was to convince the people of New York of the merits of the proposed US Constitution.

 # 68 is the second in a series of eleven essays discussing the powers and limitations of the Executive Branch but it is the only essay to describe the method of selecting a president using the Electoral College.

Constitutional debates

The Constitutional Convention was a series of one debate after another. The method of selecting the president was no exception.

The objective was to find a way that would be agreeable to the bodies represented at the convention. Different plans were proposed, including:

The Virginia Plan: from Virginia Governor Edmund Randolph; which called for the selection of the Executive from the National Legislature.

Elbridge Gerry proposed selection by the state executives (governors).

The New Jersey plan was very similar to the Randolph/Virginia plan, but called instead for the possibility of a plural executive.

In other words, he liked the idea of a ruling committee rather than one individual as chief executive.

Hamilton initially supported a lifetime appointment for an executive, but he backed off.

James Wilson proposed a novel idea of direct election by the people, but he gained no support and for a while, it decided that the president would simply be elected by Congress, a body that had proportional state representation based on population.

When the Constitution was just about finished and in draft form, the idea of how the President should be elected came up again. Gouverneur Morris brought the debate back up and decided he too wanted the people to choose the president. James Madison agreed that the election of the people at large was the best way to go about electing the president. Madison did not rush to back the proposal however. He knew that the less populous slave states would not be influential under such a system, and so he backed the notion of an Electoral College.

Hamilton and the Electoral College

Federalist No. 68 is thus the continuation of Hamilton's analysis of the presidency, in this case the concern was with the mode of selecting the United States President. In the essay, Alexander Hamilton argues for our modern notion of the Electoral College, though he added a provision for a tie. His take in this case would be that the determination would be made in the House of Representatives. The members would vote on the election of the president.

In arguing for the use of the Electoral College, Hamilton focuses on a few arguments dealing with the use of the Electoral College instead of direct election. First, in explaining the role of the general populace in the election of the president, Hamilton justifies that the, "sense of the people", through the election of the electors to the Electoral College, should be a part of the process. The final say, however, should lies with the electors, who Hamilton notes are,

"Men most capable of analyzing the qualities adapted to the station and acting under circumstances favorable to deliberation, and to a judicious combination of all the reasons and inducements which were proper to govern their choice."

Therefore, the direct election of the president would be left up to those who have been selected by the voters to become the electors.

Why did Hamilton want an indirect election?

This indirect election is justified by Hamilton because while a Republic is still served, the system allows for only a certain type of person to be elected president, preventing individuals who are unfit for a variety of reasons to be in the position of chief executive of the country.

This is reflected in his later fears about the types of people who could potentially become president. He worries that corrupted individuals could slip into the mix—particularly those who are either more directly associated with a foreign state, or individuals. He was also worried about individuals who do not have the capacity to run the country.

The former is covered by Article II, Section 1, v of the United States Constitution, while the latter is covered by Hamilton in Federalist 68. In his essay, he notes that the person who will become president will have to be a person who possesses the faculties necessary to be a president, stating that,

"Talents for low intrigue, and the little arts of popularity, may alone suffice to elevate a man to the first honors in a single State; but it will require other talents, and a different kind of merit, to establish him in the esteem and confidence of the whole Union, or of so considerable a

portion of it as would be necessary to make him a successful candidate for the distinguished office of President of the United States"

Hamilton, while discussing the safeguards, argues that he is not concerned with the possibility of an unfit individual becoming president, instead he says,

> *It will not be too strong to say, that there will be a constant probability of seeing the station filled by characters pre-eminent for ability and virtue.*

Rules on the electors

This is Hamilton's list of specific rules for the electors. They include the following:

- The electors meet only within their own specific states to select the president.

- No individuals who have "too great devotion of the President in office"

- No individuals who currently hold elected positions within the government may serve as electors.

Selection of the vice-president

Hamilton also spent time wiring up his notion of selection for the vice president. He saw them following the same pattern as for the president, through selection by the Electoral College. He saw the US Senate as the tie breaker in an Electoral College Tie.

In #68, he also answers criticism that the Senate should have been given the power to select the vice president instead of the Electoral College.

Hamilton notes that there are two major arguments against that point: first, that the vice president's power as President of the Senate would mean that the tiebreaker of the Senate would be beholden to the Senate for his power, and therefore would be unable to make the necessary decisions as a tiebreaker without fear of removal or reprisal -- second, that the possibility of the vice president becoming president means that this individual should be elected by the people and the Electoral College, because all of the powers vested in the president could fall into the hands of the vice president.

Once you get back into these writings of the Founders, you will fully understand that they are the glue that keeps Americans free. They can help provide US all with liberty and freedom and justice forever and ever and ever... as long as we pay attention.

In this book on the Electoral College, please remember that the Founders gave a lot of thought as to how to elect a president with the least amount of potential chicanery.

Those of US, who read the Federalist Papers, though it is a somewhat arduous journey, know we have accomplished a lot. These papers—eighty-five articles written by Alexander Hamilton, John Jay, and James Madison, available for free on the Internet, quickly show US all that the Founders were very concerned that the bad aspects of any other foreign government would not become part of the new American Democratic Republic. Today's administration in Washington and some others would give the founders pause for sure.

The Founders were aware of politicians and all of their negatives; but since they never put the notion of welfare, food stamps, and cell phones in the founding documents, they did not believe that the people would permit the Republic to be tainted by notions like socialism, progressivism, Marxism, or communism.

In the early days, the people were all aware of the sacrifices the early colonists had made to secure the new America. Never in the history of man was so much patriotism shown for a nation that might not ever make it into the future.

After enduring tyranny from England and other monarchies, Americans fought for and won the revolution against England et al for the cause of liberty and freedom. So that liberty and freedom would continue as long as possible and perhaps, forever, the Founders built The Constitution.

Here we are 225 plus years later looking for hope and change rather than looking to the spirits of our Founders to rebuild our fallen country. Hope will deliver nothing when action by well spirited citizens is required but discouraged.

I have found so many people, including myself, who at one time have forgotten the many sacrifices of the revolutionaries and the gifts of freedom and liberty that were bestowed on all of US at the time of the revolutionary victory. All of these gifts have been emblazoned forever in our Constitution.

We Americans have been so blessed that we have not reminded ourselves enough over the years of our great heritage. Fourth of July celebrations are picnics, and though our parents have tried, the work of our Founders and the great Constitution they built as the basis for all our laws, is often lost in the celebration. Next boom you hear on the 4th, remember why and thank God for such brave men.

Neither freedom nor liberty come cheap so the next time an engaging politician offers you something for nothing, and in your heart, you know it is wrong; stick to your guns. Remember the words of Ben Franklin, a favorite US and Pennsylvania patriot:

"Those who desire to give up freedom in order to gain security will not have, nor do they deserve, either one." Amen!

Chapter 11   The Electoral College as Proposed by Federalist Paper # 68.

The Electoral College

It is appropriate to see again what the Founders had to say about the Federalist papers. The essay used to describe the Electoral College is Federalist Paper # 68.

This paper is reproduced in its entirety beginning on the next page:

The Federalist No. 68
The Mode of Electing the President

Independent Journal
Wednesday, March 12, 1788
[Alexander Hamilton]

To the People of the State of New York:

THE mode of appointment of the Chief Magistrate of the
United States is almost the only part of the system, of any
consequence, which has escaped without severe censure, or
which has received the slightest mark of approbation from its
opponents. The most plausible of these, who has appeared in
print, has even deigned to admit that the election of the
President is pretty well guarded.1 I venture somewhat further,
and hesitate not to affirm, that if the manner of it be not perfect,
it is at least excellent. It unites in an eminent degree all the
advantages, the union of which was to be wished for.E1

It was desirable that the sense of the people should operate in
the choice of the person to whom so important a trust was to be
confided. This end will be answered by committing the right of
making it, not to any pre-established body, but to men chosen
by the people for the special purpose, and at the particular
conjuncture.

It was equally desirable, that the immediate election should be
made by men most capable of analyzing the qualities adapted to
the station, and acting under circumstances favorable to
deliberation, and to a judicious combination of all the reasons
and inducements which were proper to govern their choice. A
small number of persons, selected by their fellow-citizens from
the general mass, will be most likely to possess the information
and discernment requisite to such complicated investigations.

It was also peculiarly desirable to afford as little opportunity as possible to tumult and disorder. This evil was not least to be dreaded in the election of a magistrate, who was to have so important an agency in the administration of the government as the President of the United States. But the precautions which have been so happily concerted in the system under consideration, promise an effectual security against this mischief. The choice of several, to form an intermediate body of electors, will be much less apt to convulse the community with any extraordinary or violent movements, than the choice of one who was himself to be the final object of the public wishes.

And as the electors, chosen in each State, are to assemble and vote in the State in which they are chosen, this detached and divided situation will expose them much less to heats and ferments, which might be communicated from them to the people, than if they were all to be convened at one time, in one place.

Nothing was more to be desired than that every practicable obstacle should be opposed to cabal, intrigue, and corruption. These most deadly adversaries of republican government might naturally have been expected to make their approaches from more than one quarter, but chiefly from the desire in foreign powers to gain an improper ascendant in our councils.

How could they better gratify this, than by raising a creature of their own to the chief magistracy of the Union? But the convention have guarded against all danger of this sort, with the most provident and judicious attention. They have not made the appointment of the President to depend on any preexisting bodies of men, who might be tampered with beforehand to prostitute their votes; but they have referred it in the first instance to an immediate act of the people of America, to be exerted in the choice of persons for the temporary and sole purpose of making the appointment.

And they have excluded from eligibility to this trust, all those who from situation might be suspected of too great devotion to the President in office. No senator, representative, or other person holding a place of trust or profit under the United States, can be of the numbers of the electors.

Thus without corrupting the body of the people, the immediate agents in the election will at least enter upon the task free from any sinister bias. Their transient existence, and their detached situation, already taken notice of, afford a satisfactory prospect of their continuing so, to the conclusion of it.

The business of corruption, when it is to embrace so considerable a number of men, requires time as well as means. Nor would it be found easy suddenly to embark them, dispersed as they would be over thirteen States, in any combinations founded upon motives, which though they could not properly be denominated corrupt, might yet be of a nature to mislead them from their duty.

Another and no less important desideratum was, that the Executive should be independent for his continuance in office on all but the people themselves. He might otherwise be tempted to sacrifice his duty to his complaisance for those whose favor was necessary to the duration of his official consequence. This advantage will also be secured, by making his re-election to depend on a special body of representatives, deputed by the society for the single purpose of making the important choice.

All these advantages will happily combine in the plan devised by the convention; which is, that the people of each State shall choose a number of persons as electors, equal to the number of senators and representatives of such State in the national government, who shall assemble within the State, and vote for some fit person as President.

Their votes, thus given, are to be transmitted to the seat of the national government, and the person who may happen to have a majority of the whole number of votes will be the President. But as a majority of the votes might not always happen to centre in one man, and as it might be unsafe to permit less than a majority to be conclusive, it is provided that, in such a contingency, the House of Representatives shall select out of the candidates who shall have the five highest number of votes, the man who in their opinion may be best qualified for the office.

The process of election affords a moral certainty, that the office of President will never fall to the lot of any man who is not in an eminent degree endowed with the requisite qualifications. Talents for low intrigue, and the little arts of popularity, may alone suffice to elevate a man to the first honors in a single State; but it will require other talents, and a different kind of merit, to establish him in the esteem and confidence of the whole Union, or of so considerable a portion of it as would be necessary to make him a successful candidate for the distinguished office of President of the United States.

It will not be too strong to say, that there will be a constant probability of seeing the station filled by characters pre-eminent for ability and virtue. And this will be thought no inconsiderable recommendation of the Constitution, by those who are able to estimate the share which the executive in every government must necessarily have in its good or ill administration. Though we cannot acquiesce in the political heresy of the poet who says:

"For forms of government let fools contest --
That which is best administered is best," --yet we may safely pronounce, that the true test of a good government is its aptitude and tendency to produce a good administration.

The Vice-President is to be chosen in the same manner with the President; with this difference, that the Senate is to do, in respect to the former, what is to be done by the House of Representatives, in respect to the latter.

The appointment of an extraordinary person, as Vice-President, has been objected to as superfluous, if not mischievous. It has been alleged, that it would have been preferable to have authorized the Senate to elect out of their own body an officer answering that description. But two considerations seem to justify the ideas of the convention in this respect. One is, that to secure at all times the possibility of a definite resolution of the body, it is necessary that the President should have only a casting vote.

And to take the senator of any State from his seat as senator, to place him in that of President of the Senate, would be to exchange, in regard to the State from which he came, a constant for a contingent vote. The other consideration is, that as the Vice-President may occasionally become a substitute for the President, in the supreme executive magistracy, all the reasons which recommend the mode of election prescribed for the one, apply with great if not with equal force to the manner of appointing the other. It is remarkable that in this, as in most other instances, the objection which is made would lie against the constitution of this State.

We have a Lieutenant-Governor, chosen by the people at large, who presides in the Senate, and is the constitutional substitute for the Governor, in casualties similar to those which would authorize the Vice-President to exercise the authorities and discharge the duties of the President.

PUBLIUS

1. Vide Federal Farmer.
E1. Some editions substitute "desired" for "wished for".

Chapter 12 Throw the Bums Out!

Write opinion letters and call your representatives

The purpose of this book as noted from the beginning is to help us all be better Americans by understanding the Constitution along with America's founding—especially as it pertains to the Electoral College.

Most of us have seen or read or heard parts of the Constitution and if they have been presented properly, we more than likely, really like them.

The Constitution is the defining document of our country. It is the place to go to find out what America is all about! It is about the U.S. of A.—our nation. Our Country is what it is—because its definition is embodied in the Constitution, America's most fundamental set of laws.

Our job, moving through life, of course, as citizens of this great country, is to learn what we can about our government (as defined by the Constitution). In this endeavor, we should all pay attention that our representatives actually spend their time representing US according to the laws of the Founders.

When our representatives do not do the will of the people in-between elections we need to write letters to the editors of newspapers and other media, and write our Congressmen and Senators so they know they cannot snooker us.

If they don't listen, then we must do the honorable thing and write them even more letters, and letters to the editors. And when they choose not to respond in our favor, we then must un-elect our leaders their next time out on the ballot.

Un-elect them! They would hate it!

Unfortunately for Americans, our representative in the Congress, the Supreme Court, and the Presidency is not Jefferson Smith from the movie Mr. Smith Goes to Washington. His honor was impeccable. But, the honor of our representatives is quite questionable.

Our representation has been getting progressively worse each year—not better. Over the past few years, since 2009 through 2016, especially with the healthcare debacle, it is clear that the voices of the people have not been heard in Washington, DC.

Just as Jefferson Smith in the Frank Capra classic movie, Mr. Smith Goes to Washington, found out, the corrupt purposes of elected officials is now in the open. It is to serve themselves by serving special interests.

In the sunlight of the day, therefore, the existing Congress—yes, both houses must go. Not the institution of Congress, just the corrupt members who choose not to serve the people.

We must bid them sayonara. We must say adieu.

Prior to the November 2016 election, more Americans than ever before seemed to be tuned in to the high stakes the election represented. People were fed up with many Democratic members of Congress as well as a number of Republicans. Almost the whole country was fed up with the President but the corrupt press kept quoting approval ratings that were unbelievable.

And, so, throngs of people came out and voted for Donald Trump, who was the anti-establishment candidate for both major Parties. Trump is now our President elect but as we have been discussing in this book, there is still a lot of whining going on about recounts and the popular vote.

Ladies and Gentlemen of America, we must keep doing this. The job is not complete and it may not be complete until honesty is the American default. We the people must enforce honesty from this day forward.

If the mess we have today was not the intentions of the president of the last eight years, and if liberal progressives suggest the mess is not his direct fault, then whose fault, I might ask, is it? Might it be Stanley Laurel's or Oliver Hardy's—for it surely it would be a comedy if it were not such a tragedy.

Surprise in today's email

Before I get to this email, I got another surprise again today, hoping to remove all errors from this book through an extensive editing process. Before I show you the picture and the remarks I received, I have to tell you that I was shopping at Malacari's, a great low-price produce market in Wilkes-Barre PA today when I was joking around with both the checkout person and the person behind me. I admitted that I was unemployed but I did not say I was writing books hoping the big ship would one day come in. Hah!

I said that I was thinking about running for President but it seems that everybody is so happy with the current president (Obama at the time) that I figure I will have to look someplace else for employment. I then said that everybody loves him so much, I would not have a chance.

The cashier stopped in her tracks and said that may have been a while ago but you should check again; it is not that way now.

The lady behind her said that she did not think anybody liked him anymore. I have relatives in my family who are still doing well and they still love the president, so I figured the president was still doing OK. But, when these Jane Q Publics told me they were retired and collecting and still felt they had to work 'til they died, I started to think maybe you can't fool all of the people all of the time. It is encouraging that more and more people are beginning to think. It is also great that people are no longer afraid to talk about it.

In the same vein, I got another surprise from a famous artist and a magnificent painting that I show below. On Kindle, it is in color.

This is the intro to this email before I show you the picture. It is not current but it was new for me.

Dear John,

I thought this an interesting fw – so true.

From: Trish
Sent: Saturday, June 07, 2014 9:39 AM
To: great people
Subject: RE: New Painting

If you are familiar with Jon McNaughton's paintings, you will love this one.

This is his latest---his opinions on the current situation are stated very clearly by his paintbrush and his comments below, but no comment is really needed.

McNaughton felt compelled to add text to his painting as follows:

Many Americans today feel a sense of dismay and horror as we see our country in a downward spiral; economically, morally, and politically. President Obama's indifferent attitude and the continuous list of scandals and bad policy are leading the country to ruin. As an artist I am reminded of the old saying "Nero fiddled while Rome burned." History believes that Nero himself may have set the great fire that burned a part of Rome during his leadership. Afterwards, he blamed it on the Christians who suffered great persecution under his rule. I see great similarities to what we are experiencing today. Obama fiddled, while the people witnessed the demise of America. ***Jon McNaughton***

Again, it is not my intent to cast aspersions on the president. My purpose is to teach about that part of the Constitution that describes the Electoral College, but all of these perspectives help us all.

For the last eight years, my books have always helped Americans know what to do to escape from under the yoke of this president and his lawlessness. Now, thankfully, the people are in charge again and we now have a great leader, Donald Trump who is holding the reins from January 20, 2017 for eight glorious and prosperous years.

Look at McNaughton's painting and you get it clearly. America has been falling apart and we all decided to save it.

The email explained immediately below is also reflective of today's major problems.

Every now and then, we all get encouraged when somebody speaks out exactly how we all should be speaking out. It is what it is.

I'll let the emails that I received speak for themselves.

Here is another:

Sent from my iPad

Begin forwarded message:
From: Roger
To: undisclosed-recipients:
Subject: Fwd: FW: Two Americas

Two Americas

To add balance to the president's speech last night, read the below;

This is as well said as anything I have seen. Take the time to read it. No matter your political affiliation, Democrat, Republican, or Independent, it should be clear that this country is in a lot of trouble. Some of us will live long enough to see the consequences, but I really fear for our children and grandchildren's future. The damage that can and will be done over the next three years (at the time Obama had three years left) will likely be irreversible or take years to overcome.

In early January 2014, Bob Lonsberry, a Rochester talk radio personality on WHAM 1180 AM, said this in response to Obama's "income inequality speech":

To Americans

The Democrats are right, there are two Americas.

The America that works, and the America that doesn't. The America that contributes, and the America that doesn't. It's not the haves and the have not's, it's the do's and the don'ts. Some people do their duty as Americans, obey the law, support themselves, contribute to society, and others don't. That's the divide in America.

It's not about income inequality, it's about civic irresponsibility. It's about a political Party that preaches hatred, greed and victimization in order to win elective office. It's about a political Party that loves power more than it loves its country. That's not invective, that's truth, and it's about time someone said it.

The politics of envy was on proud display a couple weeks ago when President Obama pledged the rest of his term to fighting "income inequality." He noted that some people make more than other people that some people have higher incomes than others, and he says that's not just.

That is the rationale of thievery. The other guy has it, you want it, Obama will take it for you. Vote Democrat. That is the philosophy that produced Detroit. It is the electoral philosophy that is destroying America.

It conceals a fundamental deviation from American values and common sense because it ends up not benefiting the people who support it, but a betrayal. The Democrats have not empowered their followers;

they have enslaved them in a culture of dependence and entitlement, of victimhood and anger instead of ability and hope.

The president's premise - that you reduce income inequality by debasing the successful - seeks to deny the successful the consequences of their choices and spare the unsuccessful the consequences of their choices.

Because, by and large, income variations in society is a result of different choices leading to different consequences. Those who choose wisely and responsibly have a far greater likelihood of success, while those who choose foolishly and irresponsibly have a far greater likelihood of failure. Success and failure usually manifest themselves in personal and family income.

You choose to drop out of high school or to skip college - and you are apt to have a different outcome than someone who gets a diploma and pushes on with purposeful education. You have your children out of wedlock and life is apt to take one course; you have them within a marriage and life is apt to take another course. Most often in life our destination is determined by the course we take.

My doctor, for example, makes far more than I do. There is significant income inequality between us. Our lives have had an inequality of outcome, but, our lives also have had an inequality of effort. While my doctor went to college and then devoted his young adulthood to medical school and residency, I got a job in a restaurant.

He made a choice, I made a choice, and our choices led us to different outcomes. His outcome pays a lot better than mine.

Does that mean he cheated and Barack Obama needs to take away his wealth? No, it means we are both free men in a free society where free choices lead to different outcomes.

It is not inequality Barack Obama intends to take away, it is freedom. The freedom to succeed, and the freedom to fail. There is no true option for success if there is no true option for failure.

The pursuit of happiness means a whole lot less when you face the punitive hand of government if your pursuit brings you more happiness than the other guy. Even if the other guy sat on his arse and did nothing. Even if the other guy made a lifetime's worth of asinine and shortsighted decisions.

Barack Obama and the Democrats preach equality of outcome as a right, while completely ignoring inequality of effort.

The simple Law of the Harvest - as ye sow, so shall ye reap - is sometimes applied as, "The harder you work, the more you get." Obama would turn that upside down. Those who achieve are to be punished as enemies of society and those who fail are to be rewarded as wards of society.

Entitlement will replace effort as the key to upward mobility in American society if Barack Obama gets his way. He seeks a lowest common denominator society in which the government besieges the successful and productive to foster equality through mediocrity.

He and his Party speak of two Americas, and their grip on power is based on using the votes of one to sap the productivity of the other. America is not divided by the differences in our outcomes, it is divided by the differences in our efforts. It is a false philosophy to say one man's success comes about unavoidably as the result of another man's victimization.

What Obama offered was not a solution, but a separatism. He fomented division and strife, pitted one set of Americans against another for his own political benefit. That's what socialists offer. Marxist class warfare wrapped up with a bow.

Two Americas, coming closer each day to proving the truth to Lincoln's maxim that a house divided against itself cannot stand."

Wow! Isn't that why you are reading this book? Thank you Bob Lonsberry! We need more of you in our America!

Another thoughtful Email

I just got this today, a few days before the book will be printed.

From: <Smithy from Kingston>
Date: Sun, 4 Dec 2016 10:59:14 -0500
X-Mailer: Microsoft Windows Live Mail 16.4.3528.331
This is quite interesting and makes a great point.

There are 3,141 counties in the United States.
Trump won 3,084 of them.
Clinton won 57.

There are 62 counties in New York State.
Trump won 46 of them.
Clinton won 16.

Clinton won the popular vote by approx. 1.5 million votes.

In the 5 counties that encompass NYC, (Bronx, Brooklyn, Manhattan, Richmond & Queens) Clinton received well over 2 million more votes than Trump. (Clinton only won 4 of these counties; Trump won Richmond).

Therefore these 5 counties alone, more than accounted for Clinton winning the popular vote of the entire country. These 5 counties comprise 319 square miles. The United States is comprised of 3, 797,000 square miles.

When you have a country that encompasses almost 4 million square miles of territory, it would be ludicrous to even suggest that the vote of those who inhabit a mere 319 square miles should dictate the outcome of a national election.

Large, densely populated Democrat cities (NYC, Chicago, LA, etc) don't and shouldn't speak for the rest of our country.

End of email

Appendix 1: The Founding Documents

These founding documents are downloadable on the Internet. Simply type in the title and they are free. If you want to buy a paperback book that has all of these documents in it, here are several: *Taxation Without Representation*, *America 4 Dummmies*, and *The Constitution 4 Dummmies*. These books are available at amazon.com/author/brianwkelly. The you get includes book versions available on Kindle.

These are the appendices that are available in some of my other books. This list provides a brief introduction of each of the founding documents

Appendix A: The Declaration of Rights and Grievances

At the First Continental Congress, the delegates drafted several documents, and several drafts of documents, one of which was the Declaration of Rights and Grievances. This was a statement of American complaints. It was sent to King George III, to whom, at the time, many of the delegates remained loyal. It was not sent to Parliament since the delegates did not have the same level of loyalty to this body. Quite frankly, the document implored King George III to step in and rescue the colonies from the English Parliament.

The radical delegates were critical of this particular declaration because it continued to concede the right of Parliament to regulate colonial trade, a view that was losing favor in the mid-1770s. Many suggest that the actual cause of the American Revolution is found in this major historical document.

Appendix B
The Articles of Association

Articles of Association stated that if the Intolerable Acts were not repealed by December 1, 1774, a boycott of British goods would begin in the colonies.

Appendix C
The Declaration of Independence

On July 4, 1776, the Second Continental Congress, announced that the thirteen American colonies, then at war with Great Britain, regarded themselves as 13 newly independent sovereign states, and no longer a part of the British Empire.

Appendix D
The Articles of Confederation

The Articles of Confederation was an agreement among the 13 founding states that established the United States of America as a confederation of sovereign states and served as its first Constitution.

The Articles were used as the fundamental law of the US until the Constitution was ratified.

Appendix E
The US Constitution America

The Constitution of the United States is the supreme law of the United States of America. The Constitution, originally consisted of seven articles, which delineate the national form of government.

Appendix F
The Bill of Rights & Other Constitutional Amendments

The first ten amendments to the U.S. Constitution are known as The Bill of Rights. Freedom of religion, speech, press, assembly, and petition. Overall there are twenty-seven Amendments to the Constitution and six proposed amendments that were not ratified by the states.

LETS GO PUBLISH! Books by Brian Kelly:
(sold at www.bookhawkers.com Amazon.com, and Kindle.).

My Red Hat Keeps Me On the Ground Magic: W/O my red hat I would fly

Cross Country With The Parents Another adventure with the Petru Family.

Four Dollars & Sixty-Two Cents A Christmas Story That Will Melt Your Heart!

Seniors, Social Security & Minimum Wage. Things seniors need to know.

How to Write Your First Book and Publish It with CreateSpace

The US Immigration Fix It's all in here. An answer that Americans love.

I had a Dream IBM Could be #1 Again The title is self-explanatory

Great Moments in Penn State Football Check out particulars of great book .

Great Moments in Notre Dame Football Check out this great book

WineDiets.Com Presents The Wine Diet How to lose weight & have fun.

Wilkes-Barre, PA; Return to Glory Wilkes-Barre City's return to glory

Geoffrey Parsons' Epoch... The Land of Fair Play Better than the original.

The Bill of Rights 4 Dummmies! The Best book to learn about your rights.

America 4 Dummmies Learn about America, your country

The Constitution 4 Dummmies Greatest governing document ever written

Sol Bloom's Epoch ...Story of the Constitution Learn the Constitution

America for Dummmies! All American read about greatest country.

The All-Everything Machine Story about IBM's finest computer server.

Brian has written 95 books. Others can be found at amazon.com/author/brianwkelly

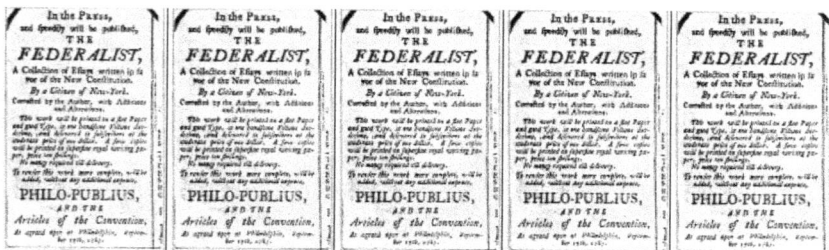

www.ingramcontent.com/pod-product-compliance
Lightning Source LLC
Chambersburg PA
CBHW070802290326
41931CB00011BA/2105